Pocket

HONG KONG

TOP SIGHTS • LOCAL LIFE • MADE EASY

Piera Chen

In This Book

QuickStart Guide

Your keys to understanding the city – we help you decide what to do and how to do it

Need to Know
Tips for a smooth trip

Neighbourhoods
What's where

Explore Hong Kong

The best things to see and do, neighbourhood by neighbourhood

Top Sights
Make the most of your visit

Local Life
The insider's city

The Best of Hong Kong

The city's highlights in handy lists to help you plan

Best Walks
See the city on foot

city' Best...
The best experiences

Survival Guide

Tips and tricks for a seamless, hassle-free city experience

Getting Around
Travel like a local

Essential Information
Including where to stay

Our selection of the city's best places to eat, drink and experience:

◎ **Sights**

✖ **Eating**

⊖ **Drinking**

✪ **Entertainment**

🔒 **Shopping**

These symbols give you the vital information for each listing:

☏ Telephone Numbers	👪 Family-Friendly
⊙ Opening Hours	🐾 Pet-Friendly
P Parking	🚌 Bus
⊖ Nonsmoking	⛴ Ferry
@ Internet Access	Ⓜ Metro
🛜 Wi-Fi Access	Ⓢ Subway
🥗 Vegetarian Selection	⊖ London Tube
📖 English-Language Menu	🚊 Tram
	🚆 Train

Find each listing quickly on maps for each neighbourhood:

Bar Hemingway

16 ⊖ Map p233, B2

Legend has it that Hemi
self, wielding a machine
borate this timber-pan
ered bar during
showpiece is a
en by Papa ar
town. Dress
s.com; Hôtel Rit
⊙6.30pm-2a

Lonely Planet's Hong Kong

Lonely Planet Pocket Guides are designed to get you straight to the heart of the city.

Inside you'll find all the must-see sights, plus tips to make your visit to each one really memorable. We've split the city into easy-to-navigate neighbourhoods and provided clear maps so you'll find your way around with ease. Our expert authors have searched out the best of the city: walks, food, nightlife and shopping, to name a few. Because you want to explore, our 'Local Life' pages will take you to some of the most exciting areas to experience the real Hong Kong.

And of course you'll find all the practical tips you need for a smooth trip: itineraries for short visits, how to get around, and how much to tip the guy who serves you a drink at the end of a long day's exploration.

It's your guarantee of a really great experience.

Our Promise

You can trust our travel information because Lonely Planet authors visit the places we write about, each and every edition. We never accept freebies for positive coverage, so you can rely on us to tell it like it is.

The Best of Hong Kong · 157

Hong Kong's Best Walks

Hong Kong's Best ...

Survival Guide · 187

QuickStart Guide

Welcome to Hong Kong

Hong Kong beckons and baffles, like the plot in one of its award-winning crime thrillers. Behind the city's futuristic facade hide smoky temples, surf-beaten beaches and sprawling, cattle-graced country parks. Hong Kong quickens the blood, yet reassures with the rule of law, an unbeatable transport system and the world's very best dim sum.

View over Wan Chai (p62) and Kowloon (p94)
IAN TROWER / AWL IMAGES LTD/GETTY IMAGES ©

Hong Kong
Top Sights

Star Ferry (p24)

At only HK$2.50, the 15-minute ride on the legendary Star Ferry, with its views of the dramatic urban coastline and the shimmering waters of Victoria Harbour, must be one of the world's best-value cruises.

PETER SCHOLEY/GETTY IMAGES ©

Tsim Sha Tsui East Promenade (p96)

This balmy promenade offers the best vantage points for viewing Hong Kong's most famous imagery: gleaming skyscrapers lined up between emerald hills and a sapphire harbour crisscrossed by ships.

WALTER BIBIKOW/GETTY IMAGES ©

KIMBERLEY COOLE/GETTY IMAGES ©

Victoria Peak (p42)

Take Hong Kong's oldest thrill ride, the Peak Tram, for an almost-vertical ascension to the summit and the Peak Tower for postcard-perfect views of the city and the harbour.

HSBC Building (p26)

Designed by architect Norman Foster, this impressive feat of high-tech modernism houses the HSBC headquarters; this monument in glass and steel is one of Hong Kong's most iconic buildings.

Man Mo Temple (p28)

This Taoist temple mesmerises with its bitter-sweet history and a smoky air infused by burning incense coils hanging from the ceiling like inverted mushrooms in a strange garden.

Temple Street Night Market (p114)

Stalls sell a myriad of booty, from alarm clocks to Nepalese daggers. Nearby, fortune tellers summon from dimly lit tents, and Cantonese opera singers strike a pose under the stars.

Happy Valley Racecourse (p64)

Even if you don't bet on the ponies, attending an electrifying Wednesday-evening meeting at this urban racecourse is one of the most exhilarating things to do in Hong Kong.

Sik Sik Yuen Wong Tai Sin Temple (p124)

This bustling temple complex is dedicated to a deified healer, and offers visual excitement, quirky landscaping, colourful Taoist ceremonies and the obligatory fortune telling.

Tian Tan Buddha (p136)

'Big Buddha' is the world's largest seated outdoor bronze Buddha. He occupies a hilltop spot on leafy Lantau Island, but you can see him also as you fly into Hong Kong on a clear day.

Ruins of the Church of St Paul (p142)

Macau's most famous landmark is, rightfully, this gorgeous facade decorated with intricate carvings and detailed engravings; it was once part of a 17th-century Jesuit church.

Hong Kong Park (p66)

A top-notch aviary; photogenic lawns, ponds and waterfalls; and an exquisite tea-ware museum housed in a colonial building are the main draws of this attractive human-made park.

Hong Kong Local Life

Insider tips to help you find the real city

Alongside the top sights, you can experience Hong Kong like a local by exploring the coolest hang-outs, the pet beaches, the favourite mountain trails and those little indulgences that make up a Hong Konger's perfect day.

LKF & Soho Bar Crawl (p46)

▶ Amphitheatre
▶ Club 71

Drinking spots frequented by Hong Kong's revered revelers: some on account of the crowd they attract, some because of the decor, and others because they could only exist in Hong Kong.

Wan Chai Breather (p68)

▶ Southorn Playground
▶ Rent-a-Curse Grannies

Life in the city can be stressful, but Wan Chai's older quarter is full of opportunities for urbanites to regain their peace of mind. These run the gamut from gadget shopping and delicious food to folk sorcery and a cemetery.

Beach-Hopping on Island South (p86)

▶ Spices Restaurant
▶ South Bay

With beaches running from West to East, the southern coast of Hong Kong Island offers a balmy bazaar, a promenade overlooking the waves, kayaking and windsurfing opportunities and, of course, fine sands and clean water.

Hiking in the New Territories (p128)

▶ Tai Long Wan Trail
▶ Shing Mun Reservoir Trail

At the first whiff of autumn, Hong Kongers make a beeline for the hills. Here are trails featuring a range of vistas – including volcanic rocks around a reservoir, emerald hills and sapphire waters, old miners' homes and a Hakka village.

Lamma Island (p138)

▶ Yung Shue Wan
▶ Lamcombe Seafood Restaurant

On laid-back Lamma, you can spend the whole day lazing on the beach with a few beers. Other possible indulgences include gorging on seafood, hiking and picnicking, even

Repulse Bay (p87)

Wan Chai street market (p83)

learning about the local fishing culture.

Exploring Taipa & Coloane Islands (p144)

▶ Taipa House Museum
▶ Chapel of St Francis Xavier

Charming temples, stilt houses, great food, a museum and an eccentric chapel are among the traditional attractions of Macau's islands of Taipa and Coloane. And if you want to play the tables, you can certainly do that too.

Other great places to experience the city like a local:

Wan Chai's Markets (p83)

Shanghai Street (p117)

Aberdeen (p93)

Happy Valley Racecourse (p64)

Yau Ma Tei's Sing-Along Parlours (p118)

Mah-Jong Parlours (p123)

Hong Kong's Trams (p72)

Kau Kee (p35)

Sheung Wan (p34)

Hong Kong
Day Planner

Day One

☼ Catch the Peak Tram up to **Victoria Peak** (p43) for stunning views of the city. Have a leisurely walk on the Peak. Once back on solid ground, head over to historic **Sheung Wan** (p22), checking out the art galleries and antique shops as you make your way westward. Stop at **Man Mo Temple** (p28) for a taste of history, and if you've already booked a tour, check out the new and wonderful **Liangyi Museum** (p32) on Hollywood Rd. Retrace your steps back east to lunch on excellent dim sum at the atmospheric **Luk Yu Tea House** (p51).

☼ Take the **Star Ferry** (p24) to Kowloon. Enjoy the views along **Tsim Sha Tsui East Promenade** (p96) as you stroll to the **Hong Kong Museum of History** (p99) for some context to your impressions of Hong Kong. Alternatively, replace the Museum of History with the **Hong Kong Museum of Art** (p97), closer to the pier.

☾ After a delicious modern Chinese dinner at **Yin Yang** (p76) in Wan Chai, take the tram to **Lan Kwai Fong and Soho** (p46) for drinks and clubbing.

Day Two

☼ Visit the lovely **Hong Kong Park** (p66) and the **Flagstaff House Museum of Tea Ware** (p67) in Admiralty. Then hop over to **Wan Chai** (p72) and explore the temples, old streets and other heritage sites on and around Queen's Rd East. Gorge on Southeast Asian delicacies at **Old Bazaar Kitchen** (p76).Take the MTR to Tsim Sha Tsui.

☼ Visit the glorious **Former Marine Police Headquarters** (p100), then amble down Nathan Rd to another two important historic buildings for a peek: **Former Kowloon British School** (p101) and **St Andrew's Anglican Church** (p99). Have afternoon tea at the **Peninsula** (p102) hotel or, if you prefer, snack on samosas while exploring **Chungking Mansions** (p100) just across the road. Browse the malls and shops in **Tsim Sha Tsui** (p110) for souvenirs.

☾ Dine al fresco at one of the *dai pai dongs* (food stalls) in the **Temple Street Night Market** (p114), followed by drinks and music at a **sing-along parlour** (p118) nearby. If you wish to continue, walk over to the **Wholesale Fruit Market** (p118) in the wee hours of the morning and watch as elderly proprietors haggle and bare-backed workmen unload boxes of fruit under the moon.

Short on time?
We've arranged Hong Kong's must-sees into these day-by-day itineraries to make sure you see the very best of the city in the time you have available.

Day Three

☀ Take the bus to Aberdeen for a **sampan cruise** (p90) of the Aberdeen Typhoon Shelter. If you're in the mood for more local fishing culture, head over to Ap Lei Chau old town and take a look inside the **Ap Lei Chau Market Cooked Food Centre** (p90). It's a wet market with some of the most diverse fresh seafood offerings in Hong Kong. Take a quick walk around the small and sleepy old town.

☀ You can lunch on simple noodles in the old town, or you can save that for the next stop. Take the bus to the multi-storey **Horizon Plaza** (p92), overlooking the typhoon shelter, to shop for off-season clothing, bargain furniture and unusual gifts. Have lunch at a cafe there if you haven't already.

☾ Have dinner at **Yè Shanghai** (p104) in Tsim Sha Tsui, then head to **Butler** (p106) in the eastern part of Tsim Sha Tsui for expensive Japanese whisky or some fancy mixology action.

Day Four

☀ Start your day with a **taichi class** (p100) by the Tsim Sha Tsui harbourfront. Invigorated, take a long stroll (or the bus) to Yau Ma Tei. Have breakfast at the deliciously retro **Mido Café** (p120). Cross the road to the atmospheric **Tin Hau Temple** (p117) and the park in front of it. Spend about 40 minutes there. Then it's on to the **Jade Market** (p117) for browsing and possibly souvenirs, and **Shanghai Street** (p117) for more browsing and local flavour.

☀ When you feel you're done with Yau Ma Tei, descend into the nearest MTR station and go to Central. Have a sumptuous Japanese lunch at **Sushi Kuu** (p51).

☾ After lunch, shop for classy Chinese-inspired gifts at **Shanghai Tang** (p39) in Central, or for well-priced electronic gadgets at **Wan Chai Computer Centre** (p82) two MTR stations away. Alternatively, you can visit a temple in Kowloon: the Taoist **Sik Sik Yuen Wong Tai Sin Temple** (p125) or the Buddhist **Chi Lin Nunnery** (p125). Have dinner at Chi Lin Vegetarian inside the latter, before heading to **Wan Chai's bars** (p78) for a final night of debauchery.

Need to Know

For more information,
see Survival Guide (p188)

Currency
Hong Kong dollar (HK$) for Hong Kong, pataca (MOP$) for Macau.

Language
Cantonese, English and Mandarin. Also Portuguese for Macau.

Visas
Not required for visitors from the US, Australia, New Zealand, Canada, the EU, Israel and South Africa for stays of up to 30 days.

Money
ATMs widely available. Credit cards accepted in most hotels and restaurants; some budget places only take cash.

Mobile Phones
Set your phone to roaming, or buy a local SIM card if you need to make lots of calls.

Time
Hong Kong Time (GMT/UTC plus eight hours).

Plugs & Adaptors
Plugs are UK-style with three square prongs. North American visitors will need an adaptor and/or transformer. Most convenience stores sell adaptors.

Tipping
Taxi drivers only expect you to round up to the nearest dollar. Many restaurants add a 10% service charge to the bill.

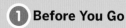

① Before You Go

Your Daily Budget

Budget less than HK$1200
▶ Guesthouse HK$150–HK$400
▶ *Cha chaan tangs* (tea houses) and *dai pai dongs* (food stalls) for food HK$60–HK$150

Midrange HK$1200–HK$2300
▶ Double room HK$900–HK$1900
▶ Chinese dinner with three dishes HK$300

Top End more than HK$2300
▶ Boutique or four-star hotel double HK$2000
▶ Dinner at top Chinese restaurant from HK$800

Useful Websites

Lonely Planet (www.lonelyplanet.com/hong-kong, www.lonelyplanet.com/china/macau) Destination info, hotel bookings etc.

Discover Hong Kong (www.discoverhong-kong.com) Tourist-authority website.

Urbtix (www.urbtix.hk) Ticket booking.

Time Out Hong Kong (www.timeout.com.hk) Events and entertainment listings.

Hong Kong Observatory (www.hko.gov.hk)

Advance Planning

Two months before Check festival dates; book lodging, concert tickets, and a table at the most popular restaurants.

One month before Check listings; book tickets to fringe festivals; research dining options.

Two weeks before Book harbour cruises, nature tours; sign up for email alerts from events organisers.

One week before Check weather forecast.

2 Arriving in Hong Kong

Fly into **Hong Kong International Airport** (HKIA; www.hongkongairport.com), or cross the border at Lo Wu or Lok Ma Chau from Shēnzhèn on mainland China by bus or train (www.mtr.com.hk). Transport to the city centre is convenient.

✈ From Hong Kong International Airport

Destination	Best Transport
Central	Airport Express; Air Bus A11
Sheung Wan, Wan Chai, Causeway Bay	Airport Express then taxi; Air Bus A11
Aberdeen and the South	Air Bus A10
Tsim Sha Tsui, Yau Ma Tei, Mong Kok	Airport Express then taxi; Air Bus A21

From Lo Wu & Lok Ma Chau border gates

Destination	Best Transport
Admiralty, Central, Tsim Sha Tsui	MTR East Line to Kwun Tong Line to Tsuen Wan Line
Sheung Wan, Wan Chai, Causeway Bay	MTR as per Central, change at Central to Island Line
Yau Ma Tei, Mong Kok	MTR East Line to Kwun Tong Line

✈ At the Airport

At Hong Kong International Airport, **Customer Services Centres** (arrivals hall ⊘7am-11pm, departures hall ⊘5am-1am) provide maps; money-exchange and banking counters; ATMs; and pay or courtesy phones. Counters at the arrivals hall help with accommodation or car hire. **Luggage storage facility** (⊘5.30-1.30am) on Level 3 of Terminal 2.

3 Getting Around

Hong Kong's efficient Mass Transit Railway (MTR) system, comprehensive bus network, and ferries will take you almost anywhere you need to go. A prepaid Octopus card can be used on most forms of public transport. MTR stations also sell one-day passes (adult/child HK$55/25) for unlimited rides on the MTR.

🚕 Taxi

Cheap compared to Europe and North America. Most are red; green ones operate in parts of the New Territories; blue ones on Lantau Island. All run on meter.

🚃 MTR

Hong Kong's MTR system covers most of the city and is the easiest way to get around. Most lines run from 6am to after midnight.

🚌 Bus

Relatively fast, they are an indispensable form of transport to places not reachable by the MTR or after midnight.

🚋 Tram

Slow but the upper deck offers great views. Runs along the northern strip of Hong Kong Island, from 6am to midnight.

⛴ Ferry

Connects Hong Kong Island and Kowloon Peninsula via Victoria Harbour. Modern ferry fleets run between Central and the outlying islands.

Hong Kong
Neighbourhoods

Temple Street
Night Market ◉

**Hong Kong Island:
Lan Kwai Fong &
Soho (p44)**
Art galleries, stylish
bars and local life as it
has been for decades
grace the streets of
Hong Kong's partying
epicentre.

Star ◉
Ferry

◉
Man Mo
Temple   ◉
            HSBC
            Building
◉   ◉
The Peak   Hong Kong
            Park

**Hong Kong Island:
Central & Sheung
Wan (p22)**
Central: high finance
meets haute couture;
Sheung Wan: temples,
antiques, dried seafood
and funeral products.

◉ **Top Sights**

Star Ferry

HSBC Building

Man Mo Temple

**Hong Kong Island:
Admiralty, Wan
Chai & Causeway
Bay (p62)**
Admiralty has a restored
explosives magazine;
Wan Chai buzzes with
markets, nightlife and
multilingual kitchens; in
Causeway Bay, shoppers
shop.

◉ **Top Sights**

Happy Valley Racecourse

Hong Kong Park

Trip to Macau (p140)

◉ **Top Sights**

Ruins of the Church of
St Paul

New Territories (p126)

Kowloon: Yau Ma Tei & Mong Kok (p112)

A famous night market and a leafy temple define Yau Ma Tei; Mong Kok offers sardine-packed commercialism.

👁 Top Sights

Temple Street Night Market

Worth a Trip

👁 Top Sights

Victoria Peak

Sik Sik Yuen Wong Tai Sin Temple

Tian Tan Buddha

👁
Tsim Sha Tsui East Promenade

Kowloon: Tsim Sha Tsui (p94)

Sophisticated, with great museums, iconic views, colonial gems and all of Central's superlatives on a more human scale.

👁 Top Sights

Tsim Sha Tsui East Promenade

👁
Happy Valley Racecourse

Hong Kong Island: Aberdeen & the South (p84)

Attractive beaches, a seafront bazaar, sampan cruises in a typhoon shelter, one of Asia's best theme parks and awesome seafood.

Explore
Hong Kong

Figurines for sale on Cat Street (p35)
PETE SEAWARD/LONELY PLANET ©

Explore

Hong Kong Island: Central & Sheung Wan

The business heart of Hong Kong, sharp-suited Central is a heady mix of exclusive boutiques, peaceful parks, gourmet dining, corporate cathedrals and historic buildings (including a real cathedral). Arguably even more rewarding to explore, Sheung Wan carries the echo of 'Old Hong Kong', with its traditional shops, Taoist temples and steep 'ladder streets', which are composed entirely of stairs.

The Sights in a Day

☀ If it's a weekday, avoid taking the MTR during the morning rush hour (7.30am to 9am). Visit **Man Mo Temple** (p28) and the temples on Tai Ping Shan St; watch elders come to light their morning incense. Explore the neighbourhood. Beat the noon-to-2pm lunch crowds by having an early bite at **Tasty Congee & Noodle Wonton Shop** (p36) before visiting the excellent **Hong Kong Maritime Museum** (p34).

☀ View classical Chinese furniture and European vanities at the **Liangyi Museum** (p32) if you've booked a tour. Shop for funky trinkets at **Cat Street** (p35). Over the next couple of hours, check out the modern and colonial-era architecture in the vicinity. Recharge at **Hong Kong Zoological & Botanical Gardens** (p33), before indulging in retail therapy at **IFC Mall** (p40).

☾ Have dinner at **Boss** (p35), followed by cocktails at **Duddell's** (p36) or **Sevva** (p38).

 Top Sights

Star Ferry (p24)

HSBC Building (p26)

Man Mo Temple (p28)

💜 **Best of Hong Kong**

Eating

Boss (p35)

Lung King Heen (p35)

Tasty Congee & Noodle Wonton Shop (p36)

Views

Bank of China Tower (p32)

Star Ferry (p24)

Two IFC (p34)

Getting There

Ⓜ **Metro** Central station (Island and Tsuen Wan lines); Hong Kong station (Airport Express); Sheung Wan station (Island line).

🚌 **Bus** Island buses stop at **Central bus terminus** (Exchange Sq); bus 26 links Central with Sheung Wan.

🚋 **Tram** Along Des Voeux Rd Central and Des Voeux Rd West.

⛴ **Star Ferry** From Tsim Sha Tsui to Central Pier 7.

Top Sights
Star Ferry

No trip to Hong Kong is complete without a ride on the Star Ferry, that fleet of electric-diesel vessels with names like *Morning Star* and *Twinkling Star*. At any time of the day the ride, with its riveting views of skyscrapers and mountains, must be one of the world's best-value cruises. At the end of the 10-minute journey, watch as a hemp rope is cast and caught with a billhook, just as it was in 1888 when the first boat docked.

Map p30, G1

天星小輪

www.starferry.com.hk

adult HK$2.50-3.40, child HK$1.50-2.10

every 6-12min, 6.30am-11.30pm

M Hong Kong, exit A2

Star Ferry

Don't Miss

Kowloon Concourse

In 1910 the Kowloon–Canton Railway was built near the Kowloon concourse, linking Hong Kong with the mainland. On Christmas Day 1941 the colonial governor took the ferry to Tsim Sha Tsui, where he surrendered to the Japanese at the Peninsula Hotel. You can still see the **Clock Tower** (前九廣鐵路鐘樓; Southern tip of Salisbury Rd, Tsim Sha Tsui Star Ferry Concourse; ⛴Star Ferry, ⓂEast Tsim Sha Tsui, exit J) of the original train station and the Peninsula here. In 1966 thousands gathered at the Kowloon concourse to protest against a fare increase. The protest erupted into the 1966 Riot, the first in a series of important social protests leading to colonial reform.

Piers

The pier on Hong Kong Island is an uninspiring Edwardian replica that was built to replace the old Edinburgh Pl pier, which was built in streamline moderne style and had a clock tower. The old pier was demolished despite vehement opposition from Hong Kong people. The Kowloon pier, resembling a finger pointing at Hong Kong Island, remains untouched.

☑ Top Tips

▶ Take your first trip from Kowloon to Central. It's more dramatic in this direction.

▶ For a surreal experience, take a ride during the nightly Symphony of Lights laser show, between 8pm and 8.20pm.

▶ If you don't mind noise and fumes, the lower deck (only open on the Tsim Sha Tsui–Central route) is better for photos.

▶ The coin-operated turnstiles take exact change or the Octopus card; you can get change from the ticket window.

✗ Take a Break

For a beer and a bite, ascend to **Pier 7** (Map p30, G1; ☎2167 8377; www.cafedecogroup.com; Shop M, Roof Viewing Deck, Central Pier 7, Star Ferry Pier, Central; ⊗9am-midnight, happy hour 6-9pm; 🛜; ⓂHong Kong, exit A1) on the rooftop viewing deck of the Star Ferry Pier; or buy snacks and drinks from the shops near Central Piers and consume while people-watching.

Top Sights
HSBC Building

The stunning HSBC headquarters, designed by British architect Norman Foster in 1985, is a masterpiece of precision, sophistication and innovation. And so it should be. On completion it was the world's most expensive building (costing more than US$1 billion). The 52-storey building reflects the architect's wish to create areas of public and private space, and to break the mould of previous bank architecture. A lighting scheme fitted later enabled the building to maintain its splendour at night.

◉ Map p30, F4

滙豐銀行總行大廈

1 Queen's Rd Central, Central

admission free

⊙ escalator 9am-4.30pm Mon-Fri, 9am-12.30pm Sat

Ⓜ Central, exit K

HSBC Building

Don't Miss

Stephen & Stitt

The two bronze lions guarding the main entrance were designed for the bank's previous headquarters in 1935. The lions are known as Stephen – the one roaring – and Stitt, after two bank employees of the time. The Japanese used the lions as target practice during the occupation; you can still see bullet holes on Stitt. Rub their mighty paws for luck.

Feng Shui

The building has unobstructed views of Victoria Harbour – water is associated with prosperity. The escalators are meant to symbolise the whiskers of a dragon sucking wealth into its belly. And they're built at an angle to the entrance to disorient evil spirits, which can only travel in a straight line.

Lighting

The 52-storey glass-and-aluminum building was installed with around 700 lighting units, including colour-changing fluorescent lights, 18 years after it was built. The project, costing $5.5 million, ensured the building dazzled as much at night as it did in broad daylight.

Atrium

The atrium, located on the 3rd floor, has greenery cascading from the different floors and is flooded with natural light. There's no prettier setting in which to get your money changed.

☑ Top Tips

▶ The ground floor is public space; you can traverse it and use the ATMs without entering the bank.

▶ Take the escalator to the 3rd floor to gaze at the cathedral-like atrium.

▶ The HSBC Building isn't Central's only iconic skyscraper; if you're an architecture buff, also check out the Bank of China Tower (p32) and Two IFC (p34).

✕ Take a Break

For million-dollar views of the HSBC Building and/or other stunners, head to the terrace of stylish restaurant and bar Sevva (p38) or the al fresco area of **Red Bar** (Map p30, G2; ☎8129 8882; www.pure-red.com; Level 4, Two IFC, 8 Finance St, Central; ◷noon-midnight Mon-Wed, to 1am Thu, to 3am Fri & Sat, to 10pm Sun, happy hour 6-9pm; 🛜; Ⓜ Hong Kong, exit E1).

Top Sights
Man Mo Temple

One of Hong Kong's oldest temples and a declared monument, atmospheric Man Mo Temple is dedicated to the gods of literature ('Man') and of war ('Mo'). Built in 1847 during the Qing dynasty by wealthy Chinese merchants, it was, besides a place of worship, a court of arbitration for local disputes in the 19th century when trust was thin between the local Chinese and the colonialists. Oaths taken at this Taoist temple (accompanied by the ritual beheading of a rooster) were accepted by the colonial government.

⊙ Map p30, C3

文武廟

☎ 2540 0350

124-126 Hollywood Rd, Sheung Wan

admission free

🕓 8am-6pm

🚌 26

Hanging incense coils, Man Mo Temple

Don't Miss

Outside the Entrance

Here are four gilt plaques on poles that used to be carried at processions. Two describe the gods being worshipped inside, one requests silence and a show of respect within the temple's grounds, and the last warns women who are menstruating to keep out of the main hall as the blood is believed to put them in a state of ritual defilement.

Main Hall

Two gold-plated sedan chairs with elaborate carvings sit here. They used to carry the statues of the deities during festivals. Lending the temple its beguiling and smoky air are rows of large earth-coloured spirals suspended from the roof, like strange fungi in an upside-down garden. These are incense coils burned as offerings by worshippers.

Lit Shing Kung

Off to the side of the main hall is 'saints' palace', built around the same time as the temple. It's a place of worship for other Buddhist and Taoist deities, including the goddess of mercy and Tai Sui, the 60 heavenly generals who each represent a particular year in the 60-year cycle of the Chinese almanac.

Kung Sor

This hall, with its name literally meaning 'public meeting place', used to serve as a court of justice to settle disputes in the Chinese community before the modern judicial system was introduced. A couplet at the entrance urges those entering to leave their selfish interests and prejudices outside.

☑ **Top Tips**

▶ The English-speaking fortune tellers (11.30am to 4.30pm, random days off) charge HK$500 to tell your fortune and HK$20 to interpret a fortune stick.

▶ You'll see a canister filled with fortune sticks in the temple. You can shake the canister, tilting it slightly, until a stick falls out. Each stick has a number corresponding to lines of text, which the fortune teller can interpret for you.

✕ **Take a Break**

Speciality tea concoctions and home-baked pastries await at **Teakha** (Map p30, B2; 茶家; ☏2858 9185; http://teakha. com; 18 Tai Ping Shan St, Shop B, Sheung Wan; ⊙11am-7pm Tue-Sun; 🛜; 🚌26), or munch on pastas and salads at **Classified the Cheese Room** (Map p30, C3; www.classifiedfoodshops. com.hk; 108 Hollywood Rd; meals HK$150-300; ⊙noon-11pm Mon-Fri, 10am-11pm Sat & Sun; 🚌26) further east.

Connaught Rd West

Des Voeux Rd West

Connaught Rd Central

A · B · C · D

1

Wilmer St

New Market St

Wing Lok St

Bonham Strand West

Ko Shing St

Sutherland St

Sheung Wan M

Queen's Rd West

Incense Shops

Queen's Rd West

Hollywood Rd

Hollywood Road Park

SHEUNG WAN

Bonham Strand East

Morrison St

Hillier St

Man Wa La

Wing Lok St

Hospital Rd

New St

Wa La La St

Sai St

Tung St

Bonham Strand East

Burd St

Jervois St

Wing Wo St

2

Po Yan St

25

3

Tai Ping Shan St

Tank La

Liangyi Museum

Cat Street

10

Gough St

X 15

Kau U Fong

Pound La

29

Po Hing Fong

Ladder St

Man Mo Temple

Bridges St

Wing Lee St

Aberdeen St

Hollywood Rd

Peel St

Gage St

Breezy Path

Bonham Rd

Seymour Rd

Shing Wong St

Staunton St

Old Bailey St

3

Park Rd

Castle Rd

SOHO

Elgin St

Chancery La

Conduit Rd

Robinson Rd

Peel St

Caine Rd

Pok Fu Lam Country Park

Shelley St

Leung Fai Tce

THE MID-LEVELS

4

Mosque St

Mosque Jct

THE PEAK

5

N

0   400 m
0   0.25 miles

E

Pier 1
Pier 2
Pier 3
Government Pier
Man Chiu St
Man Po St
Man Kwong St
Pier Rd

F

Ferries to Lamma
Pier 4
Ferries to Cheung Chau
Pier 5

G

Ferries to Launtau & Peng Chau
Pier 6

Star Ferry
Pier 7

H

VICTORIA HARBOUR

1

😊16 ✕12
Finance St

One & Two International Finance Centre ◉9

Hong Kong (Airport Express Station)

7 ◉ Hong Kong Maritime Museum
Pier 8
Pier 9

2

Ⓜ Man Cheong St
✕17 ✕13 🔒24
CENTRAL
Harbour View St

Connaught Place
Lung Wui Rd

Memorial Gardens ✕22
✕18

3

Gilman's Bazaar
Des Voeux Rd Central
Jubilee St
Victoria St
Man Yee La
Queen's Rd Central
Li Yuen St West
Li Yuen St East
Chiung Lung St
Cochrane St
Stanley St
Wellington St
Wo On La
✕11
Theatre La

🔒30

😊20

21
Connaught Garden
Connaught Place
Edinburgh Pl

Connaught Rd Central

Harcourt Rd
Murray Rd
Lambeth St
Edinburgh Pl

Ⓜ Central

LAN KWAI FONG
Wyndham St

😊28 😊27
🔒23 Duddell St
Ice House St
Lower Albert Rd

✕19
Statue Square
😊26 ◉8
Chater Rd
Former Legislative Council Building

Ice House St

HSBC Building ◉

Cheung Kong Garden
◉4
Battery Path

Chater Garden

4

Arbuthnot Rd
Glenealy
Albert Rd

Albany Rd
Upper Albert Rd
Robinson Rd

St John's Cathedral ◉

1 ◉ Bank of China Tower
Queensway

Hong Kong Zoological & Botanical Gardens ◉6

Garden Rd
Peak Tram Lower Terminus
Kennedy Rd

Cotton Tree Dr

Hong Kong Park

5

Sights

Bank of China Tower
BUILDING

1 ◎ Map p30, G4

The awesome 70-storey Bank of China Tower designed by IM Pei rises from the ground like a cube, and is then successively reduced, quarter by quarter, until the south-facing side is left to rise on its own. The public viewing gallery (open 8am to 6pm weekdays) on the 43rd floor offers panoramic views of Hong Kong. Some geomancers believe the four prisms are negative symbols; being the opposite of circles, these triangles contradict what circles suggest – money, union and perfection. (中銀大廈; BOC Tower; 1 Garden Rd, Central; Ⓜ Central, exit K)

Former Legislative Council Building
HISTORIC BUILDING

2 ◎ Map p30, G4

The colonnaded and domed building (c 1912) was built of granite quarried on Stonecutters Island, and served as the seat of the Legislative Council from 1985 to 2012. During WWII it was a headquarters of the Gendarmerie, the Japanese version of the Gestapo, and many people were executed here. Standing atop the pediment is a blindfolded statue of Themis, the Greek goddess of justice and natural law. (前立法會大樓; 8 Jackson Rd, Central; Ⓜ Central, exit G)

Liangyi Museum
MUSEUM

3 ◎ Map p30, C2

This private three-floor museum houses two exquisite collections – antique Chinese furniture from the Ming and Qing dynasties, and Chinese-inspired European vanities from the 19th and 20th century. The former is one of the world's best. The 400 pieces of precious *huanghuali* and zitan furniture are shown in rotating exhibitions that change every six months. The only way to visit is by contacting the museum at least a day in advance to join a small tour. (兩依博物館; ☑2806 8280; www.liangyimuseum.com; 181-199 Hollywood Rd, Soho; admission HK$200; ⊙10am-6pm Tue-Sat; Ⓜ Central, exit D2)

St John's Cathedral
CHURCH

4 ◎ Map p30, G4

Services have been held at this Anglican cathedral since it opened in 1849, with the exception of 1944, when the Japanese army used it as a social club. It suffered heavy damage during WWII, and the front doors were subsequently remade using timber salvaged from HMS *Tamar*, a British warship that guarded Victoria Harbour. You walk on sacred ground in more ways than one here: it is the only piece of freehold land in Hong Kong. Enter from Battery Path. (聖約翰座堂; ☑2523 4157; www.stjohnscathedral.org.hk; 4-8 Garden Rd, Central; admission free; ⊙7am-6pm; ☒12A, 40, 40M, Ⓜ Central, exit K)

AMANDA HALL/GETTY IMAGES ©

Former Legislative Council Building

Queen's Road West Incense Shops

PAPER OFFERINGS

5  Map p30, A2

At 136–150 Queen's Rd West, there are shops selling incense and paper offerings for the dead. The latter is burned to propitiate departed souls and the choice of combustibles is mindblowing – dim sum, iPads, Rolexes, Viagra tablets and, the latest: solar-powered water heaters. You may buy them as souvenirs, but remember that keeping these offerings meant for the dead (rather than burning them) is supposed to bring bad luck. (Queen's Rd W, Sheung Wan; ⊙8am-7pm; ☐26)

Hong Kong Zoological & Botanical Gardens

PARK

6  Map p30, E5

This Victorian-era garden has a collection of fountains, sculptures and greenhouses, plus a zoo and some fabulous aviaries. Along with exotic vegetation, some 160 species of bird reside here. The zoo is surprisingly comprehensive, and is one of the world's leading centres for the captive breeding of endangered species. (香港動植物公園; www.lcsd.gov.hk/parks; Albany Rd, Central; admission free; ⊙terrace gardens 5am-10pm, greenhouse 9am-4.30pm; ⋔; ☐3B, 12)

Hong Kong Maritime Museum

MUSEUM

7 ◎ Map p30, H2

This is one of the city's strongest museums, with 15 well-curated galleries detailing over 2000 years of Chinese maritime history and the development of the Port of Hong Kong. Exhibits include ceramics from China's ancient sea trade, shipwreck treasures and old nautical instruments. A painted scroll depicting piracy in China in the early 19th century is one of Hong Kong's most important historical artefacts, and, like the rest of the museum, a real eye-opener. (香港海事博物館; ☎3713 2500; www.hkmaritimemuseum.org; Central Ferry Pier 8, Central; adult/senior/child HK$30/15/15; ⊙9.30am-5.30pm Mon-Fri, 10am-7pm Sat & Sun; ♿; M Hong Kong, exit A2)

Statue Square

SQUARE

8 ◎ Map p30, G4

This leisurely square used to house effigies of British royalty. Now it pays tribute to a single sovereign – the founder of HSBC. In the northern area (reached via an underpass) is the **Cenotaph** (和平紀念碑; Chater Rd), built in 1923 as a memorial to Hong Kong residents killed during the two world wars. On the south side of Chater Rd, Statue Sq has a pleasant collection of fountains and seating areas, with tiling that's strangely reminiscent of a 1980s municipal washroom. (皇后像廣場; Edinburgh Pl, Central; M Central, exit K)

One & Two International Finance Centre

BUILDING

9 ◎ Map p30, F2

These pearl-coloured colossi resembling electric shavers sit atop the Interna-

---

Understand

Walls in Sheung Wan

In the 19th century many Chinese flocked to Hong Kong from the mainland in search of employment. The majority were coolies who settled in Sheung Wan. Afraid they'd get too close to the Europeans living nearby, the British imposed a segregation policy: Chinese to the west, Europeans to the east, with Aberdeen St serving as the invisible wall between the two. Conditions in the Chinese quarter were atrocious. The British turned a blind eye, and a bubonic plague broke out in 1894, killing 20,000 people.

From the time of the plague until after WWII, other walls were erected in Sheung Wan. To prevent landslides on steep Hong Kong Island, masonry workers shored up many slopes adjacent to main roads with stone retaining walls. Open joints between the stones allowed strong species such as Chinese banyans to sprout, further strengthening the walls. Today, Sheung Wan is one of Hong Kong's most cosmopolitan areas, but the 'wall trees' are still there.

tional Finance Centre (IFC) Mall (p40). Two IFC is the tallest building on Hong Kong Island. You can't get to the top, but you can get pretty high up by visiting the Hong Kong Monetary Authority Information Centre, which has a library and exhibitions. There are half-hour guided tours daily from Monday to Saturday. (國際金融中心; One IFC, 1 Harbour View St; Two IFC, 8 Finance St, Central; Ⓜ Hong Kong, exit A2 or F)

Cat Street STREET

10 ◉ Map p30, C2

Just north of (and parallel to) Hollywood Rd is Upper Lascar Row, aka 'Cat Street', a pedestrian-only lane lined with antique and curio shops and stalls selling found objects, cheap jewellery, and newly minted ancient coins. It's a fun place to trawl through for a trinket or two, but expect most of the memorabilia to be mass-produced fakes. (摩囉街; Upper Lascar Row, Sheung Wan; ⊙ 9am-6pm; 🚍 26)

Eating

Boss MODERN CANTONESE $$$

11 ⨯ Map p30, E3

Awarded one Michelin star, the Boss is a perfectionist. Flawless service, austere modern decor, and a meticulous kitchen point to high expectations being imposed. The old-school Cantonese dishes are impressive, notably the deep-fried chicken pieces with home-fermented shrimp paste,

Century-Long Noodles

Nothing warms the soul like a bowl of hearty beef brisket (牛腩, *ngau laam*) noodles from famous **Kau Kee** (Map p30, D2; 九記牛腩; ☎ 2850 5967; 21 Gough St, Sheung Wan; meals from HK$40; ⊙ 12.30-7.15pm & 8.30-11.30pm Mon-Sat; Ⓜ Sheung Wan, exit E2). And the locals clearly know it – during the 90-odd years of the shop's existence, film stars, tycoons and politicians have joined the queue for a table. Besides regular brisket, you can order the chewier butterfly brisket (爽腩; *song laam*), and beef tendon (牛筋; *ngau gun*), served in a curry sauce with noodles.

and the baked-crab casserole. Dim sum, made with first-rate ingredients, is available at lunch. (波士廳; ☎ 2155 0552; www.theboss1.com; Basement, 58-62 Queen's Rd Central, Central; meals from HK$500; ⊙ 11.30am-midnight Mon-Sat, from 11am Sun; 🛜; Ⓜ Central, exit D2)

Lung King Heen CANTONESE, DIM SUM $$$

12 ⨯ Map p30, F2

The world's first Chinese restaurant to receive three stars from the Michelin people, still retains them. The Cantonese food, though by no means peerless in Hong Kong, is excellent in both taste and presentation, and when combined with the harbour views and the impeccable service, provides a truly stellar dining experience. The signature steamed lobster and scallop dumplings sell out early. (龍景軒; ☎3196 8888; www.fourseasons.com/hongkong; 8 Finance St, Four Seasons Hotel, Central; set lunch/dinner HK$500/1560; ◷noon-2.30pm & 6-10.30pm; 🛜; Ⓜ Hong Kong, exit E1)

Tasty Congee & Noodle Wonton Shop
NOODLES $

13 🍴 Map p30, F2

This clean and affordable eatery in the ultra-posh IFC Mall has a long line at lunch time. So learn from the ladies of leisure – shop first, eat later. Delayed gratification also means you'll be able to sample more of the Michelin-crowned deliciousness – shrimp wontons, prawn congee, stir-fried flat noodles with beef... (正斗粥麵專家; ☎2295 0101; www.tasty.com.hk; Shop 3016, Podium Level 3, IFC Mall, 1 Harbour View St, Central; dishes HK$90-200; ◷11am-10.45pm; Ⓜ Hong Kong, exit E1)

Duddell's
CANTONESE $$$

Light Cantonese fare served in riveting spaces enhanced by artwork – a graceful dining-room awash in diffused light; a marble-tiled salon in modernised '50s chic; a leafy terrace. Saturday brunch (HK$588; served noon to 3.30pm) with free-flowing champagne and all-you-can-eat dim sum is a welcome treat, especially given the usually petite serving portions. Duddell's (see **23** 🔒 Map p30; F4) is also an art gallery holding regular exhibitions and talks. (都爹利會館; ☎2525 9191; www.duddells.co; 1 Duddell St,

Level 3 & 4 Shanghai Tang Mansion, Central; lunch HK$500-800, dinner HK$800-1600; ◷noon-2.30pm & 6-10.30pm Mon-Sat; 🛜; Ⓜ Central, exit G)

Tim's Kitchen
CANTONESE $$

14 🍴 Map p30, C2

This two-floor restaurant is considered one of Hong Kong's best – as evidenced by the Michelin honour and the praises lavished by local gourmands. It serves masterfully executed Cantonese fare over two clean, modern and well-illuminated floors. Signature dishes such as the crab claw poached with wintermelon (HK$250) require preordering. Reservations essential. (桃花源; ☎2543 5919; 84-90 Bonham Strand, Sheung Wan; lunch HK$130-500, dinner HK$300-1300; ◷11.30am-3pm & 6-11pm; ♿; Ⓜ Sheung Wan, exit A2)

Chairman
CANTONESE $$$

15 🍴 Map p30, D2

Understated faux-retro decor and warm service impart a homely feel at this upmarket place serving Cantonese classics with a healthy twist. Ingredients are sourced locally; cured meat and pickles are made in their own farm. The website even has a manifesto! No surprise, almost all the dishes hit all the right notes, from flavour to presentation. Reservation absolutely essential. (大班樓; ☎2555 2202; www.thechairmangroup.com; 18 Kau U Fong, Sheung Wan; lunch/dinner from HK$200/560; ◷noon-3pm & 6-11pm; 🛜; Ⓜ Sheung Wan, exit E2)

Understand

British Colonisation & Its End

Until European traders imported opium into Hong Kong, it was an obscure backwater in the Chinese empire. The British developed the opium trade aggressively and by the start of the 19th century were trading this 'foreign mud' for Chinese tea, silk and porcelain.

Opium Wars

China's attempts to end the opium trade gave Britain a pretext for military action; gunboats were sent in. In 1841 the Union Jack was hoisted on Hong Kong Island, and the Treaty of Nanking, which ended the so-called First Opium War, ceded the island to the British crown 'in perpetuity'.

At the end of the Second Opium War in 1860, Britain took possession of Kowloon Peninsula, and in 1898 a 99-year lease was granted for the New Territories.

Transformation

Through the 20th century Hong Kong grew in fits and starts. Waves of refugees fled China for Hong Kong. Trade flourished, as did British expat social life, until Japan crashed the party in 1941.

By the end of WWII Hong Kong's population had plummeted. But trouble in China again saw refugees push the population beyond 2 million. This, together with a UN trade embargo on China during the Korean War and China's isolation, enabled Hong Kong to reinvent itself as one of the world's most dynamic ports and manufacturing and financial-service centres.

Return of Sovereignty

In 1984 Britain agreed to return Hong Kong to China in 1997, on the condition it would retain its free-market economy and its social and legal systems for 50 years. On 1 July 1997 the British era ended.

In March 2012 Leung Chun-ying became Hong Kong's fourth chief executive. Leung's so-far unsubstantiated 'red' connections worry many Hong Kongers, a concern exacerbated by the city's spiralling living costs and the influx of mainland tourists whose habits are very different from those of Hong Kongers.

On 1 July 2014, the 17th anniversary of the return of sovereignty, over 500,000 Hong Kong citizens took to the streets in a peaceful march demanding universal suffrage and the resignation of Leung.

Top Tip

Fine Dining the Cheap Way

To enjoy Central's gourmet European restaurants without breaking the bank, go for the lunch special menus. Some high-end places may even serve breakfast and/or afternoon tea, or sell gourmet sandwiches at a takeaway station. Book ahead if you're dining in for lunch.

Caprice   MODERN FRENCH $$$

16   Map p30, F2

In contrast to its opulent decor, Caprice, with two Michelin stars, has a straightforward menu. The meals are masterfully crafted from ingredients flown in daily from France. The selections change, but experience says anything with duck, langoustine or pork belly is out of this world. Their artisanal cheeses, imported weekly, are the best you can get in Hong Kong. (☎3196 8888; www.fourseasons.com/hongkong; Four Seasons Hotel, 8 Finance St, Central; set lunch/dinner from HK$540/1740; ☺noon-2.30pm & 6-10.30pm; ☎; Ⓜ Hong Kong, exit E1)

Tim Ho Wan, the Dim Sum Specialists   DIM SUM $

17   Map p30, F2

Opened by a former Four Seasons chef, Tim Ho Wan was the first ever budget dim sum place to receive a Michelin star. Many relocations and branches later, the star is still tucked snugly inside their tasty tidbits, including the top-selling baked barbecue pork bun.

Expect to wait 15 to 40 minutes for a table. (添好運點心專門店; ☎2332 3078; 8 Finance St, Shop 12a, Hong Kong Station, Podium Level 1, IFC Mall, Central; dishes HK$50; ☺9am-8.30pm; Ⓜ Hong Kong, exit E1)

City Hall Maxim's Palace   DIM SUM $

18   Map p30, G3

This 'palace' offers the quintessential Hong Kong dim sum experience. It's cheerful, it's noisy, and it takes place in a huge kitschy hall with dragon decorations and hundreds of locals. A dizzying assortment of dim sum is paraded on trolleys the old-fashioned way. There's breakfast on Sunday from 9am but people start queuing for a table at 8.30am. (美心皇宮; ☎2521 1303; 1 Edinburgh Pl, 3rd fl, Lower Block, Hong Kong City Hall, Central; meals from HK$150; ☺11am-3pm Mon-Sat, 9am-3pm Sun; ☎♿; Ⓜ Central, exit K)

Drinking

Sevva   COCKTAIL BAR

19   Map p30, F4

If there was a million-dollar view in Hong Kong, it'd be the one from the balcony of ultra-stylish Sevva – skyscrapers so close you can see their arteries of steel, with the harbour and Kowloon in the distance. At night it takes your breath away. To get there though, you have to overcome expensive drinks and patchy service. (☎2537 1388; www.sevva.hk; 10 Chater Rd, 25th fl, Prince's Bldg, Central; ☺noon-midnight Mon-Thu, to 2am Fri & Sat; ☎; Ⓜ Central, exit H)

Liberty Exchange

SPORTS BAR

20 Map p30, F4

This American bar and bistro beckons with open frontage, generous pourings, and a casual atmosphere. No surprise then that it's hugely popular with the bankers and hedgies who work in the vicinity. On a Friday evening, it's packed with people exchanging industry gossip over cocktails, wine or beer, or watching sports on one of the big TV screens. (☎2810 8400; www.lex.hk; 8 Connaught Pl, Two Exchange Sq, Central; ⊙noon-11.30pm Mon-Sat, to 5.30pm Sun, happy hour 3-8pm, to 5.30pm Sun; 🛜; Ⓜ Hong Kong, exit A1)

Entertainment

Grappa's Cellar

LIVE MUSIC

21 ⭐ Map p30, F3

For at least two weekends a month, this subterranean Italian restaurant morphs into a jazz or rock music venue – chequered tablecloths and all. Call or visit the website for event and ticketing details. (☎2521 2322; www.elgrande.com.hk/outlets/HongKong/GrappasCellar; 1 Connaught Pl, Central; ⊙9pm-late; Ⓜ Hong Kong, exit B2)

Hong Kong City Hall

PERFORMING ARTS

22 ⭐ Map p30, G3

Built in 1962, Hong Kong City Hall is a major cultural venue, with concert and recital halls and a theatre. (☎2921 2840, bookings 2734 9009; www.cityhall.gov.hk; 5 Edinburgh Place; Ⓜ Central, exit J3)

Shopping

Shanghai Tang

CLOTHING, HOMEWARE

23 🔒 Map p30, F3

This elegant four-level store is the place to go if you fancy a body-hugging *qipao* (cheongsam) with a modern twist, a Chinese-style clutch or a mandarin jacket. Custom tailoring is available; it takes two weeks to a month and requires a fitting. Shanghai Tang also stocks cushions, teapots, even mah-jong tile sets, designed in a modern chinoiserie style. (上海灘; ☎2525 7333; www.shanghaitang.com; 1 Duddell St, Shanghai Tang Mansion, Central; ⊙10.30am-8pm; Ⓜ Central, exit D1)

Ⓠ Local Life

Hankering for Pampering?

If you ever need balm for your traveller's feet, visit **Ten Feet Tall** (Map p30, E2; ☎2971 1010; www.tenfeettall.com.hk; 139 Queen's Rd Central, 20th & 21st fl, L Place, Central; ⊙11am-midnight Mon-Thu, 10.30am-1.30am Fri & Sat, 10.30am-12.30am Sun; Ⓜ Central, exit D2), which offers indulgences from foot reflexology and shoulder massage, to hard-core pressure-point massage and aromatic oil treatments. Or try ultra-high-end **Spa at the Four Seasons** (Map p30 F2; ☎3196 8900; www.fourseasons.com/hongkong/spa.html; Four Seasons Hotel, 8 Finance St, Central; ⊙8am-10pm; Ⓜ Hong Kong, exit F), with its comprehensive range of beauty, massage and health treatments.

Fook Ming Tong Tea Shop

DRINK

24 Map p30, F2

Tea-making accoutrements and carefully chosen teas of various ages and grades are available here, from gunpowder to Nanyan Ti Guan Yin Crown Grade – costing anything from HK$10 to HK$9000 per 100g. (福茗

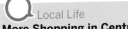

Local Life

More Shopping in Central

Sumptuous temples to couture abound inside Central's swish shopping malls, where you'll also find midrange clothing brands. Take your pick from the **Princes Building** (Map p30, F3; 太子大廈; 📞 2504 0704; www.centralhk.com; 10 Chater Rd, Central; M Central, exit K), the **Landmark** (Map p30, F3; 置地廣場; 📞 2525 4142; www.centralhk.com; 1 Pedder St, Central; M Central, exit G) or the **IFC Mall** (Map p30, F2; 📞 2295 3308; www.ifc.com.hk; 8 Finance St; M Hong Kong, exit F). **Peddar Building** (Map p30, F3; 12 Peddar St, Central; M Central, exit H) is good for fine art, while **Stanley Street** is the spot for quality cameras. **Li Yuen Street East and West** (Map p30, E3; Hong Kong Island; ⏰ 10am-7pm; M Central, exit C), two narrow alleyways that link Des Voeux Rd Central with Queen's Rd Central, has a jumble of inexpensive clothing, handbags and jewellery.

堂; 📞 2295 0368; www.fookmingtong.com; 8 Finance St, Shop 3006, Podium Level 3, IFC Mall, Central; ⏰ 10.30am- 8pm Mon-Sat, 11am-8pm Sun; M Central, exit A)

Sin Sin Fine Art

ART

25 Map p30, B2

This eclectic gallery owned by a fashion designer with a flair for ethnic designs shows good-quality Hong Kong, mainland Chinese and South-east Asian art – mostly edgy paintings and photography. (📞 2858 5072; www.sinsin.com.hk; 53-54 Sai St, Sheung Wan; ⏰ 9.30am-6.30pm Mon-Sat; M Sheung Wan, exit A2)

Blanc de Chine

CLOTHING, ACCESSORIES

26 Map p30, F4

This sumptuous store specialises in Chinese men's jackets and silk dresses for women, both off-the-rack and made-to-measure. A gorgeous sequined gown takes about four weeks to make, including one fitting. If you're not in Hong Kong after a month, the shop will ship it to you. (源; 📞 2104 7934; www.blancdechine.com; 10 Chater Rd, Shop 123, Prince's Bldg, Central; ⏰ 10.30am-7.30pm Mon-Sat, noon-6pm Sun; M Central, exit H)

Armoury

MEN'S CLOTHING

27 Map p30, F4

The Armoury can help any man look like a dapper gentleman, whatever your build – the elegant shop is a specialist in refined men's wear sourced from around the world. You can choose from British, Italian and Asian-tailored suits, and a high-quality selection of shoes and ties to match. Still not good enough? Ask about their bespoke suits and custom footwear. (🕿2804 6991; www.thearmoury.com; 307, 3rd fl, Pedder Bldg, 12 Pedder St, Central; ⏰11am-8pm Mon-Sat; Ⓜ Central)

Joyce

CLOTHING, ACCESSORIES

28 🔒 Map p30, F4

This multi-designer store is a good choice if you're short of time rather than money: Marc Jacobs, Comme des Garçons, Chloé, and several of the hottest Hong Kong fashion designers are just some of the brands you'll find here. For the same duds at half the price, visit **Joyce Warehouse** (🕿2814 8313; 2 Lee Wing St, 21st fl, Horizon Plaza Arcade, Ap Lei Chau; ⏰closed Mon) in Horizon Plaza in Ap Lei Chau. (🕿2810 1120; www.joyce.com; 16 Queen's Rd Central, ground fl, New World Tower, Central; ⏰10.30am-7.30pm; Ⓜ Central, exit D1)

Gallery of the Pottery Workshop

ART, HOMEWARES

29 🔒 Map p30, B2

The gallery showcases playful ceramic objects made by local ceramic artists and artisans from the mainland and overseas. The lovely pieces range from

Queen's Road shops

crockery to sculptures. (樂天陶社; 🕿2525 7949, 9842 5889; www.potterywork-shop.com.cn; 24 Upper Station St, Sheung Wan; ⏰1-6pm Tue-Sun; 🚌26)

Hong Kong Book Centre

BOOKS

30 🔒 Map p30, F3

This basement shop has a vast selection of English-language books and magazines, particularly business titles. (🕿2522 7064; www.hongkongbookcentre.com; 25 Des Voeux Rd, Basement, On Lok Yuen Bldg, Central; ⏰9am-6.30pm Mon-Fri, to 5.30pm Sat; Ⓜ Central, exit B)

Top Sights
Victoria Peak

Getting There

🚌 **Bus** 15 to the summit; bus 15C or 12S to Peak Tram Lower Terminus.

🚋 **Tram** Peak Tram Lower Terminus, 33 Garden Rd, Central (single/return HK$28/40; every 10 to 15 min, 7am-midnight).

Standing at 552m, Victoria Peak is the highest point on Hong Kong Island, and the best way to reach it is by taking the gravity-defying Peak Tram, Hong Kong's oldest thrill-ride (125 years). Rising almost vertically above the high-rises nearby, Asia's oldest funicular clanks its way up the hillside to finish, after eight minutes, at the Peak Tower. On clear days and nights, the views from the summit are spectacular.

View from the Peak Lookout

Don't Miss

Peak Tram Historical Gallery

This **gallery** (free admission for passengers; ⏱7am–midnight) at the Lower Terminus introduces the Peak Tram's history. Until 1940 the tram was used exclusively by Westerners as Chinese were barred from the Peak. Unthinkable today, but it was already an improvement: in pre-tram days, Peakies' only mode of transport was sedan chairs carried by Chinese 'chairmen'.

Victoria Peak Garden

Some 500m to the northwest of the Upper Terminus, up steep Mt Austin Rd, is the site of the old governor's summer lodge, which was burned to the ground by the Japanese during WWII. The beautiful gardens have been restored and refurbished with faux-Victorian gazebos, sundials and stone pillars.

Nature Walks

It takes about 45 minutes to cover the dappled 3.5km circuit trail formed by Harlech Rd on the south, just outside the Peak Lookout, and Lugard Rd, which it runs into. A further 2km along Peak Rd leads to Pok Fu Lam Reservoir Rd. Hatton Rd on the western slope goes all the way down to the University of Hong Kong in Pok Fu Lam.

Peak Tower

This anvil-shaped **building** (凌霄閣; ☎2849 0668; 128 Peak Rd; ⏱10am-11pm Mon-Fri, 8am-11pm Sat, Sun & public holidays; 🚋Peak Tram) at the summit makes a good grandstand for views of the city. It has an outpost of **Madame Tussauds** (☎2849 6966; adult/child HK$250/180; ⏱10am-10pm), with wax likenesses of celebrities, and on Level 5, an open-air viewing terrace.

維多利亞山頂

www.thepeak.com.hk

admission free

⏱24hr

🚌Bus 15 from Central, below Exchange Sq, 🚋Peak Tram Lower Terminus

---

☑ Top Tips

▶ The seats on the right side of the tram carriage going up have better views.

▶ The Peak Galleria, adjoining the Peak Tower at the Upper Terminus, has an admission-free viewing deck.

✗ Take a Break

Head to the cozy **Peak Lookout** (太平山餐廳; ☎2849 1000; www.thepeaklookout.com.hk; 121 Peak Rd, The Peak; lunch/dinner from HK$250/350; ⏱10.30am-11.30pm Mon-Thu, to 1am Fri, 8.30am-1am Sat, 8.30am-11.30pm Sun; 🚌15, 🚋Peak Tram), at the road junction next to the Peak Tower, for solid European and British-Indian fare.

Explore

Hong Kong Island: Lan Kwai Fong & Soho

Lan Kwai Fong and Soho form the party epicentre of Hong Kong. Lan Kwai Fong is an alleyway dog-legging south and west from D'Aguilar St; as an area it also covers D'Aguilar St, Wo On Lane, Wing Wah Lane and Wyndham St. The crowd here is relatively young, middle class and cosmopolitan. Soho ('south of Hollywood Rd') has art galleries and antique shops, plus dining and drinking hotspots.

The Sights in a Day

🔆 Take the Peak Tram up to **Victoria Peak** (p43) and spend two hours there. Back down, have dim sum at the beautiful, Michelin-crowned **Luk Yu Tea House** (p51).

🔆 Browse the **art galleries and antique shops** (p58) on Hollywood Rd, taking care not to miss the **Central Police Station** (p49) and the new arts hub, **PMQ** (p49). Stock up on high-quality Chinese condiments and exotic snacks at **Kowloon Soy Company** (p61). Have tea at 1950s-style **Lan Fong Yuen** (p53) or vegan haven **Life Cafe** (p52).

🌙 Muscles sore from walking? Go for a body or foot massage at **Happy Foot Reflexology Centre** (p50). Getting kneaded works up an appetite: dine on old Cantonese dishes at **Ser Wong Fun** (p51). Spend the rest of the night bar crawling, stopping at **Socialito** (p52) for tacos to soak up the alcohol.

For a local's night out in Lan Kwai Fong and Soho, see p46.

🔍 Local Life

❤️ Best of Hong Kong

Getting There

🚌 **Bus** Bus 26 runs along Hollywood Rd.

Ⓜ **Metro** Central station (Island and Tsuen Wan lines).

Local Life
LKF & Soho Bar Crawl

Here are some of the more charismatic venues in Lan Kwai Fong
(LKF) and Soho favoured by
seasoned revellers. While some
may appeal to wine connoisseurs,
others to cocktail or culture buffs,
all of the selections command
enough charm, booze and atmosphere to give anyone a memorable
(even if not fully remembered)
night out.

❶ Amphitheatre

A **hang-out** (Wo On Lane, Lan Kwai Fong;
Ⓜ Central, exit D2) of young expats who
bring drinks here to shoot the breeze
or play Charades. Come for relief from
the crowds, and to meet people.

❷ Japanese-Style Mixology

The impeccably mannered Ayako runs
Japanese-style cocktail den, **Barsmith**
(☏2613 2680; www.barsmith.com.hk; 60
Wellington St, 4th fl, Lan Kwai Fong; cover

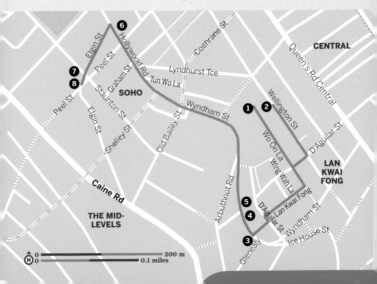

HK$200; ⊙6pm-midnight Mon-Thu, to 2am Fri & Sat; Ⓜ Central, exit D2). Ayako kneels to speak to customers when taking orders, and her cocktails are refreshingly inventive – 'Italian Bloody Mary' is made with fresh tomatoes and a drop of truffle oil.

❸ Clubby Cocktails
Stockton (☎2565 5268; www.stockton. com.hk; 32 Wyndham St, Lan Kwai Fong; ⊙6pm-late Mon-Sat; Ⓜ Central, exit D2) evokes the ambience of a private club in Victorian London. Chesterfield sofas and the odd candelabra are arranged to form intimate niches for sipping the rum- and whisky-based cocktails. Make a reservation if coming after 9pm on a weekend.

❹ Play Ball While You Drink
Skipped the gym? **Tazmania Ballroom** (☎2801 5009; www.tazmaniaballroom. com; 33 Wyndham St, 1st fl, LKF Tower, Lan Kwai Fong; ⊙5pm-late, happy hour 5-8pm; Ⓜ Central, exit D2) whips out ping-pong tables every Tuesday, Thursday and Saturday. The dress code, however, is casual glam, not Chinese national team. Shoot pool with bankers at a gold-plated table or chat up model types on the balcony.

❺ Chill, Frolic, Repeat
Sophisticated **Tivo Bar** (☎2116 8055; www.aqua.com.hk; 43-55 Wyndham St, Lan Kwai Fong; ⊙6pm-midnight Sun-Thu, to late Fri & Sat; Ⓜ Central, exit D2) delights with open frontage, aperitivo-type snacks and an exuberant crowd. On the first

and third Sunday of the month, lovely drag hostesses take over from 7pm and whip up the action for the Tivo Tea Dance.

❻ Meet Local Activists
Named after a protest on 1 July 2003 against an article that would limit freedom of speech, **Club 71** (67 Hollywood Rd, Basement, Soho; ⊙3pm-2am Mon-Sat, 6pm-1am Sun, happy hour 3-9pm; 🚍26, Ⓜ Central, exit D1) is where activists and artists gather for beer and blues jamming. Out front, revolutionaries plotted to overthrow the Qing dynasty a century ago. Enter the alley at 67 Hollywood Rd.

❼ Daiquiris in a 'Bordello'
At the end of Staunton St there's a place with velvet curtains and no signage. **Feather Boa** (☎2857 2586; 38 Staunton St, Soho; ⊙9pm-midnight Mon-Sat; 🚍26) is a romantically lit, bordello-like chamber, with gold-plated mirrors and antique furniture. The strawberry-chocolate daiquiris are popular with the European clientele. Bring ID.

❽ Craft Beer
Roundhouse Taproom (☎2366 4880; www.roundhouse.com.hk; 62 Peel St, Soho; ⊙noon-11pm, happy hour noon-8pm; Ⓜ Central, exit D1) has some of the best craft beer on tap – 25 varieties, including limited-edition beers. Pick your brew from the iPad menu and savour it inside the brightly lit bar or on the steps just outside.

Jervois St

Queen's Rd Central

SHEUNG WAN

Kau U Fong

Gough St

Mee Lun St

Aberdeen St

Gage St

Peel St

Queen's Rd Central

Gilman's Bazaar

Wellington St

27

Des Voeux Rd Central

Jubilee St

CENTRAL

Queen Victoria St

Man Yee La

Pottinger St

Li Yuen St West

Li Yuen St East

Douglas St

37
9

Stanley St

Cochrane St

Queen's Rd Central

Stanley St

PMQ 2

Hollywood Rd

19

Graham St

Gutzlaff St

13
7

15
35

SOHO

Central–Mid-Levels Escalator

Lyndhurst Tce

Wellington St

Stanley St

14
6

22
33

38

Happy Foot Reflexology Centre

4

D'Aguilar St

LAN KWAI FONG

8

21

Lan Kwai Fong

Wyndham St

17

5

Flawless Hong Kong

29

24

Caine Rd

Peel St

Elgin St

Staunton St

26
23

10

32

3
16

Ezra's La

Hollywood Rd

1

Central Police Station

THE MID-LEVELS

Old Bailey St

Chancery La

36

Arbuthnot Rd

Wyndham St

12

D'Aguilar St

Albert Rd

Glenealy

30

Caine Rd

Arbuthnot Rd

Ice House St

28
25
11
18
34
20

Elgin St

Shelley St

0 ——— 200 m
0 ——— 0.1 miles

N

For reviews see	
⊙ Sights	p49
✕ Eating	p51
🍷 Drinking	p53
☆ Entertainment	p57
🔒 Shopping	p58

PMQ

Sights

Central Police Station

HISTORIC BUILDING

1  Map p48, C3

Built between 1841 and 1919, Hong Kong's oldest symbol of law and order is this now-disused, police-magistracy-prison complex modeled after London's Old Bailey. The large compound is being redeveloped into an arts hub with cinema, museum and boutique shopping mall, due to open in 2015. (10 Hollywood Rd, Lan Kwai Fong; 🚍26, Ⓜ Central, exit D2)

Take a Break Have Hong Kong–style tea at Lan Fong Yuen (p53).

PMQ

ARTS HUB

2  Map p48, A2

This new arts hub occupies the modernist buildings and breezy courtyard of the old married police quarters (c 1951). You'll see the usual suspects – design studios, cafes, galleries and a bookstore. The site's earliest incarnation was a temple built in 1843, which was subsequently replaced by Central School, where Nationalist leader Dr Sun Yat-sen once studied. Remnants of the school remain. PMQ is bounded by Hollywood Rd (north), Staunton St (south), Aberdeen St (east), and Shing Wong St (west). (元創方; ☏2811 9098; www.pmq.org.hk;

35 Aberdeen St, S614, Block A, PMQ, Soho; ⏰9am-1pm & 2-5pm; 🚌26, Ⓜ Central, exit D2)

Central–Mid-Levels Escalator

ESCALATOR

3 ◉ Map p48, B3

The world's longest covered outdoor people mover zigzags from Central's offices to homes near Conduit Rd. Embark and let the streets unveil – Stanley and Wellington with their glamour and tradition; Gage and Lyndhurst where florists and prostitutes once hawked their wares; Hollywood, Hong Kong's second oldest street; Staunton, whose porcelain shops made way for Soho; then Shelley, named unromantically after an infamous auditor-general. (⏰down 6-10am, up 10.30am-midnight)

Take a Break Enjoy a piece of raw chocolate cake or a vegan flatbread at **Mana! Fast Slow Food** (Map p48, C3; ☎2851 1611; www.mana.hk; 92 Wellington St, Soho; meals HK$100-200; ⏰10am-10pm; 📶🍴; Ⓜ Central, exit D2)

Happy Foot Reflexology Centre

SPA

4 ◉ Map p48, D4

Foot/body massage starts at HK$200/2500 for 50 minutes. (知足樂; ☎2522 1151; www.happyfoot.hk; 1 D'Aguilar St, 19th & 20th fl, Century Sq, Lan Kwai Fong; ⏰10am-midnight; Ⓜ Central, exit D2)

Flawless Hong Kong

SPA

5 ◉ Map p48, D4

This award-winning spa attracts a youngish clientele with its homey setting, and a vast array of no-nonsense treatments for the face (from HK$980 up) and nails (manicures from HK$140). They use sophisticated 'age-combatting' and other serums, but nothing too airy-fairy like flowers or pebbles. (☎2869 5868; www.flawless.hk.com; 22-28 Wyndham St, 4th fl, Sea Bird House, Lan Kwai Fong; ⏰10am-10pm; Ⓜ Central, exit D1)

Top Tip

Budget Bites

Western fast-food chains are everywhere but for something slightly more exotic, try these local chains:

Café de Coral (www.cafedecoralfastfood.com) A huge range of Chinese dishes; free wi-fi.

Genki Sushi (www.genkisushi.com.sg) Cheap but reasonable sushi, carousel-style.

Maxim's (www.maxims.com.hk) Canto dishes with a focus on Chinese barbecued meat.

Oliver's (www.olivers-supersandwiches.com) Sandwiches and salads.

Eating

Luk Yu Tea House
CANTONESE, DIM SUM $$

6 Map p48, D3

This gorgeous teahouse (c 1933), known for its masterful cooking as well as its Eastern art-deco decor, was once the haunt of opera artists, writers and painters (including the creator of one exorbitant ink-and-brush gracing a wall), who came to give recitals and discuss the national fate. Today, some of the waitstaff who served the tousled glamourati will pour your tea in the same pleasantly irreverent manner. (陸羽茶室; ☑2523 5464; 24-26 Stanley St, Lan Kwai Fong; meals HK$300; ⏰7am-10pm, dim sum to 5.30pm; 🐾; MCentral, exit D2)

Ser Wong Fun
CANTONESE $

7 Map p48, C3

This snake-soup specialist whips up old Cantonese dishes that are as tantalising as its celebrated broth, and the packed tables attest to it. Many regulars come just for the homemade pork-liver sausage infused with rose wine – perfect over a bowl of immaculate white rice, on a red tablecloth. Booking advised. (蛇王芬; ☑2543 1032; 30 Cochrane St, Soho; meals HK$70; ⏰11am-10.30pm; MCentral, exit D1)

 Top Tip

Booking & Tipping

It's strongly advisable to book ahead in all but the cheapest restaurants, especially on Friday and Saturday nights. Most places above midrange add a 10% service charge to the bill. If the service at a top-end restaurant is outstanding, you might consider adding another 5% or 10% on top of the service charge. At midrange places, HK$5 to HK$20 is sufficient.

Sushi Kuu
JAPANESE $$

8 Map p48, D4

If you order the *omakase* ('I'll leave it to you') at this elegant sushi bar, the chef will lavish you with a multicourse meal prepared with the sweetest fruits of the sea available. Though not cheap at HK$1500 per person, it's excellent value for jet-fresh seafood of this quality. The lunch sets are also much raved about. Bookings essential. (☑2971 0180; 2-8 Wellington St, 1st fl, Wellington Pl, Lan Kwai Fong; lunch/dinner from HK$200/800; ⏰noon-11pm Mon-Thu & Sun, noon-12.30am Fri & Sat; MCentral, exit D2)

Yue Hing
DAI PAI DONG $

9 Map p48, C2

One of a gang of *dai pai dong* (food stalls) earmarked for preservation, easygoing Yue Hing reinvents the Hong Kong sandwich by topping the

Top Tip

Hong Kong–Style Street Food

On your left as you make your way down short Wo On Lane from D'Aguilar St, **Sharkie's** (鯊仔記; 2530 3232; 8-12 Wo On Lane, Lan Kwai Fong; snacks HK$5-25; 11.30am-6am; Ⓜ Central, exit D2) sells Hong Kong–style snacks, such as curry fish balls and egg waffles. Like the convenience stores in the neighbourhood, it's earned the reputation of being a 'cougar hotspot' because of its – presumably – young, hungry and male following.

usual suspects (ham, spam and egg) with peanut butter and cooked cabbage. And it works! Allow 15 minutes for preparation as these wacky wedges are made to order. (裕興; 76-78 Stanley St, Soho; meals HK$25-40; 8.15am-2pm; Ⓜ Central, exit D2)

Life Cafe
VEGETARIAN, INTERNATIONAL $

10 | Map p48, B3

Right next to the Central–Mid-Levels Escalator, Life is a vegetarian's dream, serving organic vegan salads, guilt-free desserts, and tasty dishes free of gluten, wheat, onion, garlic – you name it – over three floors stylishly decked out in reclaimed teak and recycled copper-domed lamps. The ground-floor counter has goodies to take away. (2810 9777; www.lifecafe.

com.hk; 10 Shelley St, Soho; meals HK$100; noon-10pm; Ⓜ Central, exit D1)

Vbest Tea House
CANTONESE $

11 | Map p48, A3

Tucked away on a steep street off Soho, this understated family-run restaurant serves MSG-free comfort food. The owners' children grew up on this, so you can't go too wrong. We recommend the homemade wontons and prawns with rice vermicelli. Vbest offers set lunch and set dinner for HK$80 and HK$100 respectively. (緻好茶館; 3104 0890; www.vbest. com.hk; 17 Elgin St, Soho; lunch/dinner from HK$120/200; noon-3pm & 6-11pm Mon-Sat; Ⓜ Central, exit D1)

Socialito
LATIN AMERICAN $$

12 | Map p48, C4

Beckoning with 1950s lights, Socialito's laid-back *taqueria* pays tribute to the taco stand with a tin roof and tasty tidbits. Behind a silver door is the *restaurante*, an opulent dining room worthy of old Mexico. Here in the half-light of chandeliers, gold surfaces flicker and carved wood stands guard as fashionable patrons tackle sumptuous lamb tamales and lobster tacos. (3167 7380; www.socialito.com. hk; 60 Wyndham St, Shop 2, ground fl, The Centrium, Lan Kwai Fong; taquería HK$150-300, restaurante HK$300-600; taquería noon-midnight Mon & Tue, to 2am Wed-Thu, to 3am Fri & Sat, restaurante 6-11.30pm Mon-Sat; Ⓜ Central, exit D2)

Dumpling Yuan NORTHERN CHINESE $

13 Map p48, C2

Locals and visitors from the north flock to this little shop for its nine varieties of juicy bundles of heaven more commonly known as lamb and cumin, pork and chives, egg and tomato or vegetarian dumplings. (餃子園; ☑2541 9737; 98 Wellington St; ☺11am-10.30pm Mon-Sat; ☑; ☑40M)

Yat Lok NOODLES $

14 Map p48, D3

Be prepared to bump elbows with locals at this tiny joint known for its roast goose. Anthony Bourdain gushed over the bird. Foodies prefer it to fowls from pricey 'goose specialists'. Our favourite cut is the leg, over rice or slippery rice noodles. Order it unchopped and rip it – crispy skin, tender flesh and all! (一樂燒鵝; ☑2524 3882; 34-38 Stanley St, Soho; meals HK$45-90; ☺7.30am-9pm Mon-Fri, 9am-5.30pm Sat & Sun; ⓜCentral, exit D2)

Lan Fong Yuen CAFE $

15 Map p48, B3

The rickety facade hides an entire *cha chaan tang* (tea house). Lan Fong Yuen (1952) is believed to be the inventor of the 'pantyhose' milk tea. Over a thousand cups of the strong and silky brew are sold daily alongside pork-chop buns, tossed noodles, and other hasty tasties. Watch staff work their magic while you wait for a table. (蘭芳園; ☑2854 0731, 2544 3895; 2 & 4A Gage St, Soho; meals from HK$60; cover charge HK$20; ☺7am-6pm Mon-Sat; ☑5B)

Drinking

Angel's Share Whisky Bar BAR

16 Map p48, C3

One of Hong Kong's best whisky bars, this clubby place has over 100 whiskies from the world over – predominantly Irish, but also French, Japanese and English. One of these, a 23-year-old Macallan, comes straight out of a large 180L oak barrel placed in the centre of the room. If you're hungry, there's a selection of whisky-inspired dishes. (☑2805 8388; www.angelsshare. hk; 23 Hollywood Rd, 2nd fl, Amber Lodge, Lan Kwai Fong; ☺3pm-2am Mon-Thu, to 3am Fri & Sat; ⓜCentral, exit D1)

☑️ Top Tip

For Lesbians

Hong Kong's premier lesbian organisation, **Les Peches** (☑9101 8001; lespechesinfo@yahoo.com), offers events for lesbians, bisexual women and their friends, including monthly club nights and a popular annual junk-trip flotilla event.

Central Wine Club

WINE BAR

17 Map p48, D4

If you're serious about your tipple and don't mind over-the-top modern Baroque decor, CWC is a great place to sample fine old-world wines. The bar's iPad wine list features over 500 bottles, in addition to Cognac and whisky. Blues and jazz provide the soundtrack to your evening. Nonmembers are subject to a 15% service charge. (☎2147 3448; www.thecentralwineclub.com; 22-28 Wyndham St, 3rd fl, Sea Bird House, Lan Kwai Fong; ⏰2pm-2am Mon-Fri, 4pm-2am Sat, happy hour 3-9pm; Ⓜ Central, exit D1)

Local Life

Gay-Friendly Bars

While Hong Kong's gay scene may not have the visibility of New York's, it's made huge strides. When homosexual acts between consenting adults were decriminalised in 1991, there were only a couple of speakeasies. Today there are some 30 bars and clubs. T:me (p54), in an alley off Hollywood Rd, is tiny but chic. Cocktail bar **Volume** (Map p48, A2; ☎2857 7683; 83-85 Hollywood Rd, Central; ⏰6pm-4am, happy hour 7.30-9.30pm; 🚌26) pumps out sounds ranging from '80s hits to the latest dance genres. See free monthly gay magazine **Dim Sum** (http://dimsum-hk.com) for listings.

Globe

PUB

18 Map p48, B3

Besides an impressive list of 150 imported beers, including 13 on tap, the Globe serves T8, the first cask-conditioned ale brewed in Hong Kong. Occupying an enviable 370 sq metres, the bar has a huge dining area with long wooden tables and comfortable banquettes. (☎2543 1941; www.theglobe.com.hk; 45-53 Graham St, Soho; ⏰10am-2am, happy hour 10am-8pm; Ⓜ Central, exit D1)

T:ME

GAY BAR

19 Map p48, B2

A small and chic gay bar located in a back alley off Hollywood Rd, close to Club 71; drinks are a bit on the pricey side but it has happy hour throughout the week. (☎2332 6565; www.time-bar.com; 65 Hollywood Rd; ⏰6pm-2am Mon-Sat; Ⓜ Central, exit D1)

Bar 1911

BAR

20 Map p48, B3

A small bar with fine details (including stained glass, burlwood bar, ceiling fan) and a 1920s old Hong Kong vibe. The name commemorates the year Dr Sun Yat-sen overthrew the Qing monarchy. You'll see a likeness of the man inside the bar. It's usually a tad less crowded than competitors nearby, which makes for quiet drinking. (逸日會; ☎2810 6681; http://

LONELY PLANET/GETTY IMAGES ©

Globe

www.sbs.hk/1911.html; 27 Staunton St, Soho; ⏰5pm-midnight Mon-Sat, happy hour 5-9pm; 🚇26)

Bit Point
BAR

21 🚇 Map p48, D4

Smack in the thick of the Lan Kwai Fong action, German-style Bit Point has a good selection of German beers on tap, including exclusive-to–Hong Kong Bitburger, and a sausage platter to pleasantly stoke your thirst. The amicable Eurasian owner, Cindy, is happy to give you sightseeing recommendations. (☎2523 7436; 31 D'Aguilar St,

Lan Kwai Fong; ⏰1pm-late Mon-Fri, 5pm-late Sat & Sun, happy hour 3-9pm; 🚇Central, exit D2)

Tastings
WINE BAR

22 🚇 Map p48, D3

This bar on a side street off Wellington, offers 40 wines from 'enomatic' wine dispensers that pour by a few millilitres, a half-glass or a full glass. This allows you to taste rare varietals without bankrupting yourself. You create a tab by handing over your credit card in exchange for a smart card that you use to operate the machines.

(☎ 2523 6282; www.tastings.hk; 27 & 29 Wellington St, Basement, Yuen Yick Bldg, Lan Kwai Fong; ⏱ 5pm-2am Mon-Sat; Ⓜ Central exit D2)

Dragon-I
BAR, CLUB

This fashionable venue (see **12** Map p48; C4) has both an indoor bar and a terrace over Wyndham St filled with caged songbirds. Go after midnight and watch Ukrainian models and Cantopop stars sipping Krug and air kissing, as DJs fill the dance floor with hip hop, R&B and jazz. Go early or dress to kill if you want to be let in. (☎ 3110 1222; www.dragon-i.com.hk; 60 Wyndham St, upper ground fl, the Centrium, Lan Kwai Fong; ⏱ noon-late, terrace happy hour 3-9pm Mon-Sat; 🚌 26, Ⓜ Central, exit D2)

Solas
BAR

If the nasty man wouldn't let you into Dragon-I upstairs (see **12** Map p48; C4), never mind. This relaxed, friendly, Irish-owned place, where a DJ spins chilled lounge sounds and the cocktails pack a punch, is more than a consolation prize. (Tip: Beers are better than cocktails.) (☎ 3162 3710; www.solas.com.hk; 60 Wyndham St; ⏱ 4pm-1am Mon-Fri, 6pm-1am Sat; Ⓜ Central, exit D2)

Peak Cafe Bar
BAR

This welcoming bar with great cocktails is decorated with the charming fixtures and fittings of the old Peak Cafe, from 1947, which was replaced by the Peak Lookout. The cafe comprises two parts, both next to the Central–Mid-Levels Escalator, with a courtyard linking the two. Plant yourself by the window and watch the world go by. (☎ 2140 6877; www.cafedecogroup.com; 9-13 Shelley St, Soho; ⏱ 11am-2am Mon-Fri, 9am-2am Sat, 9am-midnight Sun, happy hour 5-8pm; 🚌 13, 26, 40M)

TakeOut Comedy Club

Entertainment

Fringe Club

LIVE MUSIC, THEATRE

24 ⭐ Map p48, D5

The Fringe, housed in a Victorian building (c 1892) that was part of a dairy farm, offers original music in the **Dairy** several nights a week, with jazz, rock and world music getting the most airplay. The intimate theatres host eclectic local and international performances. The Fringe sits on the border of Lan Kwai Fong. (藝穗會; ☎2521 7251, theatre bookings 2521 9126; www.hkfringe.com.hk; 2 Lower Albert Rd, Lan Kwai Fong; ⏰noon-midnight Mon-Thu, to 3am Fri & Sat; Ⓜ Central, exits D1, D2 & G)

Peel Fresco

JAZZ

25 ⭐ Map p48, A3

Charming Peel Fresco has live jazz six nights a week, with local and overseas acts performing on a small but spectacular stage next to teetering faux-Renaissance paintings. The action starts around 9.30pm, but go at 9pm to secure a seat. (☎2540 2046; www.peelfresco.com; 49 Peel St, Soho; ⏰5pm-late Mon-Sat; 🚌13, 26, 40M)

TakeOut Comedy Club

COMEDY

26 ⭐ Map p48, A3

In need of some LOL? Hong Kong's first full-time comedy club, founded by Chinese-American Jameson Gong,

Local Life

Dance, Dance!

Even if you're here for two days, opportunities to kick up your heels abound in town. Hong Kong has a zealous community of **tango** dancers. You can join any of the milongas (dance parties) held every week; www.tangotang.com posts events. The **Hong Kong Tango Festival** (www.hktangofest.com), at the end of the year, has classes and parties.

Hong Kong's **salsa** community has weekly club nights open to anyone. See www.dancetrinity.com or www.hongkong-salsa.com. The **Hong Kong Salsa Festival** (http://hksalsafestival.com), held around February, features participants from the world over.

If you like **swing**, there are socials with live jazz bands at least six times a month. See the calendar on www.hongkongswings.com.

has stand-up and improv acts in English, Cantonese and Mandarin. It also hosts visiting comedians from overseas. See website for program. (☑6220 4436; www.takeoutcomedy.com; 34 Elgin St, Basement, Soho; ☐26)

Senses 99   LIVE MUSIC

27 ⭐ Map p48, B2

This two-floor speakeasy inside a pre-WWII building has all the features of a tasteful mid-century residence – high ceilings, balconies overlooking a quiet street, folding screen doors, and distressed couches. Music sessions begin after 10pm but before that you can take charge of the drum set and electric guitar on the 3rd floor to start a jam session or join one. (☑9466 2675; www.sense99.com; 2nd & 3rd fl, 99 Wellington St, Soho; ☺9pm-late Fri & Sat; Ⓜ Sheung Wan, exit E2)

Culture Club   LIVE MUSIC

28 ⭐ Map p48, A2

Besides the Tango milongas that take place here some Saturdays, this multipurpose venue is where amateur musicians hold their debut performances. It also features photography exhibitions, and the occasional Chinese music performance such as the blindman *nányīn* (a vanishing genre of Cantonese music). (☑2127 7936; www.cultureclub.com.hk; 15 Elgin St, Soho; ☺2.30-11.30pm; ☐26)

Shopping

Grotto Fine Art   GALLERY

29 🔒 Map p48, C5

This exquisite gallery, founded by a scholar in Hong Kong art, is one of very few that represents predominantly local artists. The small but excellent selection of works shown ranges from painting and sculpture to ceramics and mixed media. Prices are reasonable too. (嘉圖; ☑2121 2270; www.grottofineart.com; 2nd fl, 31C-D

Salsa dancing, Lan Kwai Fong

Wyndham St, Lan Kwai Fong; ⊙11am-7pm Mon-Sat; Ⓜ Central, exit D2)

Hulu 10   CLOTHING

30 🔒 Map p48

This pleasant shop sells Chinese-style tunics, jackets, dresses, and fashionably loose *qipao* (cheongsam) as worn by educated women of the 1910s. Materials have a raw feel whether it's tie-dyed cotton, patterned wool or mud-treated silk. Going uphill from the five-way intersection on Wyndham Street, the shop is on your right just before the public toilets. (☑ 2179 5500; www.hulu10.com; 10 Glenealy, Lan Kwai Fong; ⊙10am-7pm Mon-Sat; Ⓜ Central, exit D1)

Arch Angel Antiques   ANTIQUES

31 🔒 Map p48, B2

Though the specialities are ancient porcelain and tombware, Arch Angel packs a lot more into its three floors: it has everything from mah-jong sets and terracotta horses to palatial furniture. (☑ 2851 6848; 53-55 Hollywood Rd, Lan Kwai Fong; ⊙9.30am-6.30pm Mon-Sat, to 6pm Sun; 🚌 26)

Wattis Fine Art   ANTIQUES

32 🔒 Map p48, B3

The upstairs gallery here has the best collection of antique maps for sale. The selection of old photographs of Hong Kong and Macau is also impressive. Enter from Old Bailey St. (www.wattis.com.hk; 20 Hollywood Rd, 2nd fl, Lan Kwai Fong; ⏲10.30am-6pm Mon-Sat; 🚌26)

Photo Scientific

PHOTOGRAPHY

33 🔒 Map p48, D3

This is the favourite shop of Hong Kong's professional photographers. You may find cheaper equipment elsewhere, but Photo Scientific has a rock-solid reputation with labelled prices, and zero leeway for bargaining. (攝影科學; 📞2525 0550; 6 Stanley St, Lan Kwai Fong; ⏲10am-7pm Mon-Sat; Ⓜ Central, exit D2)

Top Tip
Stubbed Out

Smoking has been banned in all bars, restaurants, shopping malls, museums, public transport, and even beaches and parks in Hong Kong; but you can light up in 'al fresco' areas. Some bars, however, will risk getting fined in order to attract more customers – you know which ones they are by the ashtray nonchalantly left on tables. An exception to the ban is on cross-border trains to mainland China, where you can smoke in the restaurant car and the vestibules at either end of the cars, but not in the main seating area.

Lam Gallery

ANTIQUES

34 🔒 Map p48, B3

Arguably the best shop in the area for sculptures, this is the largest of several owned by the Lam family on Hollywood Rd. Sculpted pieces from the Neolithic period to the Qing dynasty predominate. Other products include ceramics, bronze, paintings, gold and silverware. Lam is known by collectors and auction dealers worldwide, and offers restoration services. (松心閣; 📞2554 4666; 44 Hollywood Rd, Lan Kwai Fong; ⏲10.30am-6.30pm Mon-Fri, 11am-6pm Sat; 🚌26, Ⓜ Central, exit D2)

Linva Tailor

CLOTHING, ACCESSORIES

35 🔒 Map p48, C3

Fancy a cheongsam aka *qipao* (body-hugging Chinese dress)? Bring your own silk or choose from the selection here. If you're pushed for time, the bespoke tailors, Mr and Mrs Leung, are happy to mail the completed items to you. (年華時裝公司; 📞2544 2456; 38 Cochrane St, Soho; ⏲9.30am-6.30pm Mon-Sat; 🚌26)

10 Chancery Lane Gallery

GALLERY

36 🔒 Map p48, B4

Located in Chancery Lane, this gallery focuses on thought-provoking works by promising Asian, mainland Chinese and Hong Kong artists. It also runs seminars and art walks.

10 Chancery Lane Gallery

(10 號贊善里畫廊; ☎2810 0065; www.10chancerylanegallery.com; 10 Chancery Lane, Soho; ◷10am-6pm Tue-Sat; Ⓜ Central, exit D2)

Kowloon Soy Company

CHINESE CONDIMENTS

37 Ⓐ Map p48, C2

The shop (c 1917) for artisanal soy sauce, premier cru Chinese miso, and other high-quality condiments; also sells preserved eggs (pei darn, 皮蛋) and pickled ginger (suen geung, 酸姜) which are often served together at restaurants. Did you know that preserved eggs, being alkaline, can make young red wines taste fuller-bodied? Just try

it. (九龍醬園; ☎2544 3695; www.kowloon-soy.com; 9 Graham St, Soho; ◷8am-6.15pm Mon-Fri, to 6pm Sat; Ⓜ Central, exit D1)

Lu Lu Cheung

CLOTHING

38 Ⓐ Map p48, D3

Local designer Lu Lu Cheung makes sophisticated casual wear, work clothes and evening gowns for the urban woman. There's lots of cotton, silk and linen, in whites and earth tones. The look is subtle and feminine without being prudish. (☎2537 7515; www.lulucheung.com.hk; 50 Wellington St, Lan Kwai Fong; ◷10.30am-8pm Sun-Thu, to 9pm Fri & Sat; Ⓜ Central, exit D2)

Explore

Hong Kong Island: Admiralty, Wan Chai & Causeway Bay

Quiet Admiralty offers class over quantity, whether it be shopping, sights or dining. To its east, Wan Chai is a seat of culture, a showcase for folk traditions and a nightlife guru, not to mention Hong Kong's most versatile kitchen. In the shopping hub of Causeway Bay, restaurants and department stores jockey for space with a racecourse and a cemetery.

The Sights in a Day

☀️ Pay a leisurely 2½-hour visit to **Hong Kong Park** (p66) and the **Asia Society Hong Kong Centre** (p72). Stroll through **Pacific Place** (p82) mall, browsing the shops, as you make your way back downhill. Have lunch at **La Creperie** (p69).

☀️ Spend two hours exploring the 'old Wan Chai' area: **Pak Tai Temple** (p72), **Hung Shing Temple** (p72), **Hong Kong House of Stories** (p73) and the vicinity. Continue your journey north to Hennessy Rd, shopping for gadgets at the **Wan Chai Computer Centre** (p82) and soaking up the vibes at **Southorn Playground** (p68). If you like, pay a visit to the **Hong Kong Convention & Exhibition Centre** (p74) and the **Hong Kong Arts Centre** (p74) right by the harbour. Then tram it to Causeway Bay to shop for the rest of the afternoon.

🌙 Have dinner at **Old Bazaar Kitchen** (p76) in Wan Chai, then spend the rest of the night bar-hopping in Wan Chai.

For a local's day in Wan Chai, see p68.

👁 Top Sights

Happy Valley Racecourse (p64)

Hong Kong Park (p66)

🔍 Local Life

Wan Chai Breather (p68)

💜 Best of Hong Kong

Eating

Yin Yang (p76)

Old Bazaar Kitchen (p76)

Delicious Kitchen (p77)

Irori (p77)

Drinking

Executive Bar (p78)

Pawn (p79)

Delaney's (p79)

Getting There

Ⓜ **Metro** Admiralty, Wan Chai, Causeway Bay and Tin Hau stations.

🚋 **Tram** East along Queensway, Johnston Rd and Hennessy Rd.

🚌 **Bus** Admiralty bus station below Queensway Plaza for buses around Hong Kong Island; buses 5, 5B and 26 for Yee Wo St (Causeway Bay). Green Minibus 40 along Tang Lung St and Yee Woo St (Causeway Bay).

Top Sights
Happy Valley Racecourse

Horse racing is Hong Kong's most popular spectator sport, and an evening at the races is one of the quintessential Hong Kong things to do. Every Wednesday from September to June, the Happy Valley Racecourse comes alive with eight electrifying races and an accompanying carnival of food and wine. You can try your hand at betting, or simply enjoy the collective exhilaration, the smell of the turf and the thunder of iron hoofs.

◉ Map p70, G5

跑馬地馬場

www.hkjc.com/home/english/index.asp

2 Sports Rd, Happy Valley

admission HK$10

⊙ 7pm-10.30pm Wed Sep-Jun

🚊 Happy Valley

Happy Valley Racecourse

Don't Miss

Betting

Pick up a betting slip and fill in four things: type of bet, race number, horse number(s) and amount of money you're betting (minimum is HK$10). Along with the cash, hand it to a staff member behind the betting windows at the back of the stands. You'll get a slip of paper, which you must show staff to claim your winnings after the race. Here are some basic betting types:

▶ Win – you back one horse; it wins.

▶ Place – your horse finishes first, second or third.

▶ Quinella – you choose two horses; they come first and second, in either order.

▶ Quinella place – you back any two of the first three horses.

▶ Tierce – you choose the first three horses in correct order.

▶ Trio – like the tierce, but in any order.

Tours

To know more about horseracing, consider joining the 5½-hour **Come Horseracing Tour** (☏ reservations 2316 2151; per person HK$860), run during race meetings; it includes admission to the members' area, a buffet meal and a guided tour.

Racing Museum

Racing buffs can visit the **Hong Kong Racing Museum** (Wong Nai Chung Rd, 2nd fl, Happy Valley Stand; admission free; ⏲noon-7pm, to 9pm race days; 🚋Happy Valley), which showcases celebrated trainers, jockeys and horses, and key races over the past 150 years.

☑ Top Tips

▶ Avoid crowds by leaving just before the last race. Turn right as you leave the turnstiles and walk 10 minutes to the Causeway Bay MTR station at Times Sq.

✗ Take a Break

There are high-price, decent-quality hot dogs and pizza at the racecourse. **Fiat Caffe** (Map p70, G4; www.fiat.com.hk; 77 Leighton Rd, Shop G5-G6, Leighton Centre, Causeway Bay; meals from HK$100; ⏲11am-10pm; Ⓜ Causeway Bay, exit A) offers excellent casual Italian fare served in small portions.

Top Sights
Hong Kong Park

Designed to look anything but natural, Hong Kong Park is one of the most unusual parks in the world, emphasising artificial creations such as its fountain plaza, conservatory, artificial ponds and waterfalls (a favourite of the newly-weds from the marriage registry within the park), children's playground and taichi garden. For all its artifice, the 8-hectare park is beautiful and, with a wall of skyscrapers on one side and mountains on the other, makes for dramatic photographs.

Map p70, A3

香港公園

www.lcsd.gov.hk/parks/hkp/en/index.php

19 Cotton Tree Dr, Admiralty

admission free

park 6am-11pm

Admiralty, exit C1

Hong Kong Park

Don't Miss

Edward Youde Aviary

The park's highlight, this **aviary** (尤德觀鳥園;
Hong Kong Park, Admiralty; ⏱9am-5pm; **M**Admiralty, exit
C1) is home to more than 600 birds, representing
around 90 species. Designed like a rainforest,
it has a wooden bridge suspended 10m above
the ground, eye level with tree branches. The
Forsgate Conservatory (⏱9am-5pm), on the slope
overlooking the park, is the largest in Southeast
Asia.

Flagstaff House Museum of Tea Ware

At the park's northernmost tip is this f (茶具文
物館; ☎2869 0690; www.lcsd.gov.hk/ce/museum/arts/
english/tea/intro/eintro.html; 10 Cotton Tree Dr, Admiralty;
admission free; ⏱10am-6pm Wed-Mon; **M**Admiralty, exit
C1). Built in 1846, it is the oldest colonial building
in Hong Kong still standing in its original spot.
The museum houses a collection of antique Chinese tea ware: brewing trays, sniffing cups and
teapots made of porcelain or purple clay.

KS Lo Gallery

The **KS Lo Gallery** (羅桂祥茶藝館; ☎2869 0690; 10
Cotton Tree Dr; admission free; ⏱10am-5pm Wed-Mon),
in a building southeast of the museum, contains
rare Chinese ceramics and stone seals collected
by the gallery's eponymous benefactor.

Hong Kong Visual Arts Centre

On the eastern edge of the park, the **Hong Kong
Visual Arts Centre** (香港視覺藝術中心; ☎2521
3008; www.lcsd.gov.hk/ce/Museum/Apo/en/vac.html;
7A Kennedy Rd; admission free; ⏱10am-9pm Wed-Mon),
housed in the Cassels Block of the former Victoria Barracks, supports local artists and stages
exhibitions.

☑ **Top Tips**

▶ There's a crafts
fair (noon to 6pm
Saturday and Sunday)
outside the Museum
of Tea Ware featuring
handicrafts for sale, and
calligraphy and paper-
cut art demos.

▶ Lock Cha Tea Shop
has Chinese music
performances or tea
talks on most Sunday af-
ternoons (4pm to 6pm),
but you'll need to reserve
a seat (see website for
details).

✖ **Take a Break**

Recharge over tea and
vegetarian dim sum at
classy **Lock Cha Tea
Shop** (Map p70, A3; 樂
茶軒; ☎2801 7177; www.
lockcha.com; 10 Cotton Tree
Dr, ground fl, KS Lo Gallery,
Hong Kong Park, Admiralty;
dim sum HK$15-28, tea from
HK$25; ⏱10am-10pm; ✎;
MAdmiralty, exit C1). Book
ahead if you're going
for lunch or dinner.

Local Life
Wan Chai Breather

Wan Chai is littered with hang-outs where residents or office workers go for a breather. These include not only parks, but also unlikely havens where people can let off steam or space out before checking back into the world. To visitors, these eclectic spaces offer a different side of local society and some of the best food in town.

❶ Southorn Playground

Seniors come to this **playground** (修頓球場; ⏰6am-11.30pm; Ⓜ Wan Chai, exit A3) to play chess, and students to shoot hoops and kick ball. There are hip-hop dance-offs, housewives shaking a leg, outreach social workers, cruising gays and a trickle of lunchers. Wan Chai's social hub marks the boundary between home and play. It's said that in the 1950s, sailors visiting 'Suzy Wong' bars ('hostess' bars that were

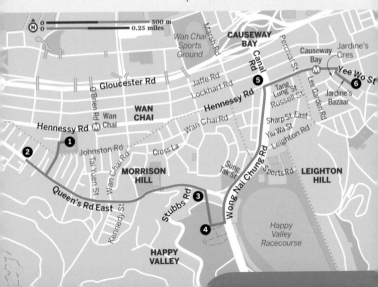

popularised by the 1960 movie *The World of Suzy Wong* starring Nancy Kwan and William Holden) will never venture beyond this playground, no matter how drunk.

❷ Crepes for Lunch

Decorated like a seaside town in Brittany, quaint 20-seat **La Creperie** (☏2529 9280; 100 Queen's Rd E, 1st fl, Wan Chai; meals HK\$70-200; ⏰11.30am-11pm Mon-Sun; Ⓜ Wan Chai, exit A3) whips out sumptuous galettes and airy crepes, which are best savoured with some imported cider served in bowls. If you fancy French andouille sausage, this creperie is one of the only places in town where you'll find that pungent delicacy.

❸ Khalsa Diwan Sikh Temple

In search of spirituality? This **temple** (☏2572 4459; www.khalsadiwan.com; 371 Queen's Rd E, Wan Chai; ⏰4am-9pm; 🚌10 from Central), built in 1901, extends its services to any caste, colour or creed. Sunday prayer (9am to 1pm) sees 1000 believers and nonbelievers in worship; fewer at the daily prayers (4am to 8am, 6pm to 8pm). It also hands out free vegetarian meals (11.30am to 8.30pm).

❹ Hong Kong Cemetery

Nearby, opposite the racecourse, this crowded Protestant **cemetery** (香港墳場; www.fehd.gov.hk/english/cc/introduc-tion.html; ⏰7am-6pm or 7pm; 🚌1, 8X, 117) lies alongside Jewish, Hindu, Muslim and Catholic cemeteries. Tombstones date to the mid-1800s and include those of tycoons, colonialists and actresses. Given dead Hong Kong's parallels with the breathing city, an escapade here may prove quite enlightening.

❺ Rent-a-Curse Grannies

Under the Canal Rd flyover near Causeway Bay, you can pay rent-a-curse grannies to punch your enemy. For HK\$50 these curse-muttering sor-ceresses will use a shoe to pound the hell out of a paper cut-out of anyone who vexes you. Villain exorcism (打小人, *da siu yan*) is believed to bring resolution.

❻ Japanese Dinner

Have dinner at cheerful **Iroha** (伊呂波燒肉; ☏2882 9877; www.iroha.com.hk; 50 Jardine's Bazaar, 2nd fl, Causeway Bay; lunch sets from HK\$110, dinner from HK\$300; ⏰noon-3pm & 6-11pm; Ⓜ Causeway Bay, exit E) in Causeway Bay. It specialises in *yakiniku*, the Japanese style of grilling food over a burner. Among the dizzying range of Wagyu cuts on offer, the beef rib finger (*nakaochi karubi*), with its perfect fat-to-meat ratio and just-right chewiness, comes highly recommended. If you love steak, be prepared to spend.

A B C D

1

2

Ⓝ 0 ___ 500 m
0 ___ 0.25 miles

Golden
Bauhinia
Square
◉ 8

Expo Dr

Lung Wui Rd

Lung Wui Rd

Tim Wa Ave

Tim Mei Ave

Tamar
Park

Expo Dr

Convention Ave

Hong Kong Convention
& Exhibition Centre   ◉ 6
23 Ⓔ

**WAN
CHAI**

Harcourt Rd

Lambeth St

Drake St

Tamar

Admiralty Ⓜ

Admiralty

Harcourt
Garden

7 ◉ Hong Kong
Arts Centre

Luard
Rd

Gloucester R⸱

Cotton
Tree Dr

**Hong
◉ Kong
Park**

ADMIRALTY

Queensway

Fenwick Pier St

Arsenal St

Jaffe Rd

Lockhart Rd

Fenwick St

28 ★

27 25 24 21
  ✕ 16   Ⓔ 26

O'Brien Rd

Ⓜ Wan
Chai

30 Ⓐ

Pacific
Place

Justice Dr

Wing
Fung St

Queen's Rd East

Anton St

Hennessy Rd

Southorn
Playground 32

Ⓐ

Thomson
Rd

Johnston Rd

Kennedy Rd

Borrett Rd

3 Asia Society
◉ Hong Kong
Centre

22
31 Ⓐ

Star St

Ship St

19
20
✕ 11

Swallow St

Lee Tung St

Spring Garden
La

Cross St

Wan Chai P⸱

1 ◉
15

Bowen Dr

Hung Shing
Temple

Old Wan Chai ◉ 4
Post Office

Hong Kong ◉
House of Stories

Bowen Rd

Lung On St

Stone Nullah
La

5
◉ 2
Pak Tai
Temple

3

4

5

For reviews see
◉ Top Sights   p64
◉ Sights   p72
✕ Eating   p76
Ⓔ Drinking   p78
★ Entertainment   p80
Ⓐ Shopping   p82

E F G H

VICTORIA HARBOUR

Causeway Bay Typhoon Shelter 1

Causeway Bay

Cross-Harbour Tunnel

Kellett Island

Cargo Handling Basin

Hung Hing Rd

10 Noonday Gun
9 2
Victoria Park

13
35
Houston St

CAUSEWAY BAY

Harbour Rd

Wan Chai Sports Ground

Tonnochy Rd
Marsh Rd

Canal Rd

Cannon St
Percival St
Jaffe Rd
Lockhart Rd

Paterson St
Gloucester Rd

37
Great George St

29

Harbour Dr

Jaffe Rd

Lockhart Rd
Marsh Rd

Causeway Bay M
34
Kai Chiu Rd
Yee Wo St 3

Foo Ming St
Lee Garden Rd
Yun Ping Rd
Pennington St

Haven St

Stewart Rd

Hennessy Rd

18

Bowrington Rd

Russell St
Sharp St East

Matheson St

36
Hysan Ave

Heard St

Wan Chai Rd

12

Yat Sin St

Yiu Wa St

Leighton Rd
Leighton Rd

CAROLINE HILL 4

17 33

Cross La
Wood Rd

MORRISON HILL

Oi Kwan Rd

Sports Rd

Wong Nai Chung Rd

LEIGHTON HILL

Broadwood Rd

Caroline Hill Rd

Wan Chai Park

Queen's Rd East

Stubbs Rd

Hau Tak La

Wong Nai Chung Rd

HAPPY VALLEY

Happy Valley Racecourse

Ventris Rd

5

Sights

Hung Shing Temple   TEMPLE

1 ⊙ Map p70, C4

Nestled in a nook on the southern side of Queen's Rd East, this narrow, dark and rather forbidding temple (c 1847) is built atop huge boulders. It was erected in honour of a deified Tang-dynasty official who was known for his virtue (important) and ability to make predictions of great value to traders (ultra-important). (洪聖古廟; 129-131 Queen's Rd E; ⊙8am-5.30pm; ☐6, 6A, Ⓜ Wan Chai, exit A3)

Pak Tai Temple   TEMPLE

2 ⊙ Map p70, D5

A short stroll up Stone Nullah Lane takes you to a majestic Taoist temple built in 1863 to honour a god of the sea, Pak Tai. The temple – the largest on Hong Kong Island – is impressive. The main hall contains a 3m-tall copper likeness of Pak Tai cast in the Ming dynasty. (北帝廟; 2 Lung On St, Wan Chai; ⊙8am-5pm; Ⓜ Wan Chai, exit A3)

Take a Break Try **Capital Cafe** (Map p70, E4; 華星冰室; ☑2666 7766; 6 Heard St, Shop B1, ground fl, Kwong Sang Hong Bldg, Wan Chai; meals HK$35-50; ⊙7am-11pm; Ⓜ Wan Chai, exit A2) for scrambled eggs, ham and macaroni, and other Hong Kong classics.

Asia Society Hong Kong Centre   HISTORIC BUILDING

3 ⊙ Map p70, B4

An architectural feat, this magnificent site integrates 19th-century British

---

Understand
Chug Chug Ding A Ling

Nicknamed 'ding dings' by locals, trams have been sedately chugging back and forth between the Eastern and Western districts of the island since 1904. More than a century on, the world's largest fleet of double-decker tramcars – and Hong Kong's most low-carbon transport option – continues to negotiate pathways through the city's heavy traffic.

Board a 'ding ding' and watch the city unfold like a carousel of images as you relax and ponder tomorrow's itinerary. Viewing the districts east of Causeway Bay from a moving tram, moreover, imparts a cinematic quality that seeing these primarily residential districts on foot may not. Add speed to housing-block uniformity and you get rhythm and pattern. The district is served by around 30 stops on the eastbound tramline.

The bonus of riding on a tram is that you can hop off whenever something tickles your fancy. It's fun, too. High fives between passengers on passing vehicles are not unheard of.

military buildings, including a couple of explosives magazines, and transforms them into an exhibition gallery, a multipurpose theatre, an excellent restaurant and a bookstore, all open to the public. The architects Tod Williams and Billie Tsien eschewed bold statements for a subdued design that deferred to history and the natural shape of the land. The result is a horizontally oriented site that offers an uplifting contrast to the skyscrapers nearby. (亞洲協會香港中心, Hong Kong Jockey Club Former Explosives Magazine; ☎2103 9511; www.asiasociety.org/hong-kong; 9 Justice Dr, Admiralty; ⊙gallery 11am-5pm Tue-Sun, to 8pm last Thu of month; ⓜAdmiralty, exit F)

Take a Break Recharge with excellent tapas (book ahead if going for lunch or dinner) at the centre's restaurant, **Ammo** (Map p70, B4; ☎2537 9888; www.ammo.com.hk; 9 Justice Dr, Asia Society Hong Kong Centre, Admiralty; meals HK$200-400; ⊙noon-midnight Sun-Thu, to 1am Fri & Sat; ⓜAdmiralty, exit F).

Old Wan Chai Post Office

BUILDING

4 ◎ Map p70, D5

A short distance to the east of Wan Chai Market is this tiny colonial-style building erected in 1913 and now serving as a resource centre operated by the **Environmental Protection Department** (☎2893 2856; ⊙10am-5pm Mon-Tue & Thu-Sat, 10am-1pm Wed, 1-5pm Sun). (舊灣仔郵政局; 221 Queen's Rd E, Wan Chai; ⊙10am-5pm Wed-Mon; 🚌6, 6A)

Hung Shing Temple

Hong Kong House of Stories

MUSEUM

5 ◎ Map p70, D5

Opened by local residents and fans of Wan Chai, this tiny museum is in the historic **Blue House** (72-74a Stone Nullah Lane), a prewar building with cast-iron Spanish balconies reminiscent of New Orleans. The not-for-profit museum sells local handicrafts and runs private tours in English. Send an email a month in advance to arrange. A two-hour tour is HK$600 so the more of you, the cheaper. (香港故事館; ☎2835 4372; http://houseofstories.sjs.org.hk; 74 Stone Nullah Lane, Wan Chai; ⊙11am-5pm; 🚌6, 6A)

Local Life

Wan Chai's Upright Artists' Village

Foo Tak Building (Map p70, F3; 富德樓; 365 Hennessy Rd; Ⓜ Wan Chai, exit A2) was built in 1968 as a residential building, but in the 2000s its landlady turned the property into an art village. Among its 14 storeys are the studios and/or living quarters of artists, activists, indie film groups, publishers and musicians, who rent the 46-sq-metre units for a small sum of money.

Hong Kong Convention & Exhibition Centre
BUILDING

6 ◎ Map p70, D2

Due north of the Wan Chai MTR station, the massive Convention & Exhibition Centre, which was built in 1988 and extended onto an artificial island in the harbour for the official ceremony of the return of sovereignty to China in 1997, has been compared with a bird's wing, a banana leaf and a lotus petal. It's a leading venue for large trade fairs, exhibitions and conventions. (香港會議展覽中心; ☎ 2582 8888; www.hkcec.com.hk; 1 Expo Dr, Wan Chai; 🚌 18)

Hong Kong Arts Centre
BUILDING

7 ◎ Map p70, C3

Along with theatres, including the **agnès b. Cinema** (☎ 2582 0200; Upper Basement, Hong Kong Arts Centre, 2 Harbour Rd; 🚌 18), the Hong Kong Arts Centre contains the two-floor **Pao Sui Loong**

& Pao Yue Kong Galleries (包玉剛及包兆龍畫廊, 包氏畫廊; admission free; ◷ 10am-6pm, to 8pm during exhibitions), which hosts retrospectives and group shows in all visual media, several boutiques, an art bookstore, and a cafe. (香港藝術中心; www.hkac.org.hk; 2 Harbour Rd, Wan Chai; Ⓜ Admiralty, exit E2)

Golden Bauhinia Square
MONUMENT

8 ◎ Map p70, D1

A 6m-tall statue of Hong Kong's symbol stands on the waterfront just in front of the Hong Kong Convention & Exhibition Centre to mark the establishment of the Hong Kong Special Administrative Region (SAR) in 1997. The flag-raising ceremony, held daily at 8am and conducted by the Hong Kong police, is a must-see for mainland tourist groups. There's a pipe band on the first day of each month at 7.45am. (金紫荊廣場; 1 Expo Dr, Golden Bauhinia Sq, Wan Chai; 🚌 18, Ⓜ Wan Chai, exit A5)

Victoria Park
PARK

9 ◎ Map p70, H2

Victoria Park is the biggest patch of public greenery on Hong Kong Island. The best time to go is on a weekday morning, when it becomes a forest of people practising the slow-motion choreography of taichi. The park becomes a flower market a few days before the Chinese New Year. It's also worth a visit during the **Mid-Autumn Festival**, when people turn out

Understand

Pollution in Hong Kong

- -

Air Quality

Hong Kong's most pressing environmental problem is air pollution, responsible for up to 2000 premature deaths a year. Not surprisingly, it has become a highly charged political and economic issue. Mounting public pressure has forced the government to take more decisive measures in recent years to control emissions from vehicles and power plants, the major source of air pollution. Government statistics show that the emission of most air pollutants has gone down, except sulphur dioxide, thanks to increased coal-burning by power plants. That said, many travellers to Hong Kong might find it hard to breathe in congested areas such as Causeway Bay and Mong Kok.

The Hong Kong Special Administrative Region (SAR) government's new Air Quality Health Index (AQHI) monitors Hong Kong's air quality and alerts the public to potential health risks posed by excessive exposure to air pollutants through a website (www.aqhi.gov.hk/tc.html) and mobile application.

Waste

Three large landfills in the New Territories absorb all of Hong Kong's daily 16,500 tonnes of municipal waste (though they will soon be full). As space for building large landfills is limited, the government introduced waste reduction schemes in 1998, but progress has been slow. Only 40% of household waste is recycled.

Looking Ahead

The future of Hong Kong's environment will depend not only on the city's efforts, but also on whether pollution in the greater Pearl River Delta region is tamed. The most polluted water in Hong Kong is found in Deep Bay, which is shared with nearby Shēnzhèn, and Hong Kong's air quality deteriorates drastically when winds bring pollution from the north. The governments of Hong Kong and Guǎngdōng are working together to tackle regional pollution. Though progress has been slow, their success will bring a greener Hong Kong and Pearl River Delta.

en masse carrying lanterns. (維多利亞公園; www.lcsd.gov.hk/en/ls_park.php; Causeway Rd, Causeway Bay; admission free; ⏱6am or 7am-11pm; Ⓜ Tin Hau, exit B)

Take a Break Head to the classy **Dickens Bar** (Map p70, H2; www.mandarinoriental.com/excelsior/dining/dickens_bar; 281 Gloucester Rd, Basement, Excelsior Hong Kong, Causeway Bay; ⏱noon-1am Mon-Fri, to 2am Fri & Sat, happy hour 4-8pm; Ⓜ Causeway Bay, exit D1) for ale and British pub grub.

Noonday Gun
HISTORIC SITE

10 ◎ Map p70, H2

A colonial tradition dating back to the mid-1800s, the daily firing of this Hotchkiss 3-pounder naval gun was made famous by the Noël Coward song 'Mad Dogs and Englishmen' ('In Hong Kong, they strike a gong, and fire off a noonday gun/To reprimand each inmate who's in late'). The gun stands in a small garden opposite the Excelsior Hotel on the waterfront, where its noon-on-the-dot firing always draws a small crowd. (香港怡和午炮; 221 Gloucester Rd, Causeway Bay; ⏱7am-midnight; Ⓜ Causeway Bay, exit D1)

Eating

Yin Yang
CHINESE $$$

11 Map p70, C4

Margaret Xu, the chef of Yin Yang, calls her cooking New Hong Kong. A former ad-agency owner who taught herself how to cook, Margaret grows her own organic vegetables and uses old-fashioned tools, such as stone-grinds and terracotta ovens, to create Hong Kong classics with a clean, contemporary twist. (鴛鴦飯店; ☏2866 0868; www.yinyang.hk; 18 Ship St, Wan Chai; lunch from HK$180, chef's menu dinners HK$580-2000; ⏱noon-2.30pm Sun, dinner by reservation; Ⓜ Wan Chai, exit B2)

Old Bazaar Kitchen
SINGAPOREAN, MALAYSIAN $

12 ✕ Map p70, F4

The short menu of tasty Singaporean, Malaysian and Chinese dishes at this unpretentious eatery are executed with more flair than authenticity, but it's convincing. The chef's knack for working magic with culinary influences has won him a huge following among foodies. Try the ox tongue dishes and the noodles. (老巴剎廚房; ☎2893 3998; 207 Wan Chai Rd; lunch/dinner from HK$50/150; ☺noon-4.30pm, 6-10.30pm Mon-Sat; Ⓜ Wan Chai, exit A2)

Delicious Kitchen   SHANGHAINESE $

 13 Map p70, H2

The Shanghainese rice cooked with shredded Chinese cabbage is so good at this *cha chaan tang* (tea house) that fashionistas are tripping over themselves to land a table here. It's best with the legendary honey-glazed pork chop. Fat, veggie-stuffed wontons and perfectly crispy fried tofu are also winners. (☎2577 7720; 9-11B Cleveland St, Causeway Bay; meals HK$40-100; ☺11am-11pm; Ⓜ Causeway Bay, exit E)

Irori   JAPANESE $$

14 Map p70, G4

Irori's versatile kitchen turns out raw and cooked delicacies of an equally impressive standard. Seasonal fish is flown in regularly from Japan, and carefully crafted into sushi and sashimi. To warm the stomach between cold dishes, there's a creative selection of tasty tidbits, such as fried beef roll and *yakitori* (grilled skewers). (酒處; ☎2838 5939; Yiu Wa St, 2nd fl, Bartlock Centre, Causeway Bay; lunch/dinner from HK$150/300; ☺noon-3pm & 6-11pm; Ⓜ Causeway Bay, exit A)

Ho Hung Kee   NOODLES $

The tasty noodles, wontons and congee at this 68-year-old shop (see 34 Map p70; G3) are cooked according to the ancient recipes of the Ho family, and clearly they still work. Though the new location, inside shiny Hysan Place mall, lacks character. Ho Hung Kee is always packed during lunch, even before it was awarded one Michelin star. (何洪記; ☎2577 6558; 500 Hennessy Rd, 12th fl, Hysan Place, Causeway Bay; wonton soup HK$53; ☺11.30am-11.30pm; Ⓜ Causeway Bay, exit F2)

22 Ships   TAPAS $

15 Map p70, C4

The star of the recent crop of new tapas restaurants to open in Hong Kong, this tiny, trendy spot is packed from open to close. But the long wait (the restaurant doesn't take reservations) is worth it for exquisite, playful small plates by much-buzzed-about young British chef Jason Atherton. (☎2555 0722; www.22ships.hk; 22 Ship St, Wan Chai; tapas HK$68-178; ☺noon-3pm & 6-11pm; Ⓜ Wan Chai, exit B2)

 Top Tip

Green Dining

When having seafood, avoid eating deepwater fish and shark's fin. The World Wildlife Fund (WWF) has a sustainable seafood guide you can download (www.wwf.org.hk/en/whatwedo/footprint/seafood/sci/guide/).

Che's Cantonese Restaurant
CANTONESE $$

16 Map p70, C3

This Cantonese restaurant, favoured by suits, serves home-style dishes and a small but delectable selection of dim sum. The crispy barbecued pork bun is a clever take on the *char siu bao*. The decor is simple but tables are a tad too close for comfort. (車氏粵菜軒; ☑2528 1123; 54-62 Lockhart Rd, 4th fl, The Broadway, Wan Chai; meals HK$180-800; ◷11am-3pm & 6-11pm; Ⓜ Wan Chai, exit C)

Hang Zhou Restaurant
CHINESE $$

17 Map p70, E4

A critics' favourite, this one-Michelin-star establishment excels at Hángzhōu cooking, the delicate sister of Shanghainese cuisine. Dishes such as shrimps stir-fried with tea leaves engage all your senses. (杭州酒家; ☑2591 1898; 178-188 Johnston Rd, 1st fl, Chinachem Johnston Plaza; HK$200-800; ◷11.30am-2.30pm & 5.30-10.30pm; Ⓜ Wan Chai, exit A5)

Gun Gei Healthy Vegetarian
CHINESE, VEGETARIAN $

18 Map p70, F3

This *dai pai dong* (food stall) makes simple but delicious vegetarian dishes. There are more choices at dinner, but you'll need a Chinese-speaker to book a table and pre-order dishes. The lunch special has three dishes, one soup and as much rice as you need. (根記健康素食; ☑2575 7595; 21 Bowrington Rd, No 6 Bowrington Rd Market & Cooked Food Centre, Wan Chai; HK$32-70; ◷8.30am-2.30pm, 5.30-9.30pm Mon-Sat; ☑; Ⓜ Causeway Bay, exit A)

Bo Innovation
CHINESE $$$

19 Map p70, C4

This self-identified 'X-Treme' restaurant takes classic Chinese dishes apart and reassembles them in surprising ways using the sci-fi techniques of molecular gastronomy. The pork dumpling is a wobbly blob of ginger-infused pork soup encased in a transparent wrapper that explodes in the mouth. The 'Dead Garden' dish of various fungi with green onions and avocados is characteristically surreal. The lift entrance is at 18 Ship St. (厨魔; ☑2850 8371; www.boinnovation.com; 60 Johnston Rd, 2nd fl, Wan Chai; lunch set/tasting menu HK$288/780, dinner tasting menu HK$1380-2180; ◷noon-2pm Mon-Fri, 7-10pm Mon-Sat; Ⓜ Wan Chai, exit B2)

Drinking

Executive Bar
LOUNGE

You won't be served if you just turn up at this clubby, masculine bar high above Causeway Bay (see 14 Map p70; G4) – it's by appointment only. Odd perhaps, but worth the trip if you are serious about whisky and bourbon. Several dozen varieties are served here, in big brandy balloons with large orbs of ice hand-chipped by the Japanese proprietor to maximise the tasting experience. (☑2893 2080; 3 Yiu Wa St, 7th fl, Bartlock Centre, Causeway Bay; ◷5pm-1am Mon-Sat; Ⓜ Causeway Bay, exit A)

Pawn

BAR

20  Map p70, D4

This handsome three-storey establishment used to be a row of tenement houses and the century-old Woo Cheong pawn shop. Now it's occupied by a restaurant and a bar. The slouchy sofas with space to sprawl, shabby-chic interiors designed by a filmmaker, plus great little terrace spaces overlooking the tram tracks, make this an ideal location to sample a great selection of lagers, bitters and wine. (www.thepawn.com.hk; 62 Johnston Rd, Wan Chai; 11am-2am, to midnight Sun; M Wan Chai, exit A3)

Delaney's

BAR, PUB

21 Map p70, D3

This popular Irish watering hole has a black-and-white-tiled pub on the ground floor and a sports bar and restaurant on the 1st floor. The food is good and plentiful; the kitchen allegedly goes through 400kg of potatoes a week. (www.delaneys.com.hk; 18 Luard Rd, ground & 1st fl, One Capital Place, Wan Chai; noon-3am, happy hour noon-9pm; M Wan Chai, exit C)

Classified

CAFE

22 Map p70, C4

We love the scrubbed wooden table, the designer lamp and the open frontage of this quiet and stylish cafe. Take a seat near the pavement and people-watch as you enjoy your pick from 100+ bottles and some quality tapas. (2528 3454; 31 Wing Fung St, Admiralty; 8am-midnight; M Admiralty, exit F)

Dim sum

Champagne Bar

BAR

23 Map p70, D3

Take your fizz in the sumptuous surrounds of the Grand Hyatt's Champagne Room, kitted out in art-deco furnishings to evoke Paris of the 1920s. Live blues or jazz happens most evenings and the circular main bar is always busy. (1 Harbour Rd, ground fl, Grand Hyatt Hotel, Wan Chai; 5pm-2am; M Wan Chai, exit A1)

Mes Amis

BAR

24 Map p70, D3

A slightly more stylish place in the lap of girly club land, Mes Amis has a list of Mediterranean-style snacks and a good range of wines. There's a DJ from 11pm on Friday and Saturday. (✆2527 6680; www.mesamis.com.hk; 81-85 Lockhart Rd, Wan Chai; ⏲noon-4am Sun-Thu, to 6am Fri & Sat, happy hour 4-9pm; Ⓜ Wan Chai, exit C)

Amici
SPORTS BAR

25 Map p70, C3

The champion of Wan Chai sports bars features ample screens, five beers on tap, decent American-Italian food and a long happy hour. A few local football supporters' clubs have made Amici their base, and it's easy to see why. The atmosphere during live broadcasts of big sporting events is contagious. (www.amicihongkong.com; Lockhart Rd, 1st fl, Empire Land Commercial Centre, Wan Chai; ⏲noon-1am Sun-Thu, to 2am Fri & Sat; Ⓜ Wan Chai, exit C)

Agave
BAR

26 Map p70, D3

Fans of tequila will be ecstatic here – there are 170 brands of the spirit, and the bartenders are heavy-handed with it. Interiors are brightly coloured with cactus-themed adornments and jovial atmosphere. (www.epicurean.com.hk; 93 Lockhart Rd, Shop C & D, Wan Chai; ⏲noon-1am Sun-Thu, to 2am Fri & Sat, happy hour 3-9pm; Ⓜ Wan Chai, exit C)

Carnegie's
PUB

27 Map p70, C3

The rock memorabilia festooning the walls makes it all seem a bit Hard Rock Café-ish, but this place is worth a look all the same. From 9pm on Friday and Saturday, Carnegie's fills up with young revellers, many of whom will end up dancing on the bar which has brass railings in case they fall. (www.carnegies.net; 53-55 Lockhart Rd, ground fl, Wan Chai; ⏲11am-late Mon-Thu, from noon Sat, from 5pm Sun, happy hour 11am-9pm Mon-Sat; Ⓜ Wan Chai, exit C)

Entertainment

Hong Kong Arts Centre
DANCE, THEATRE

The Hong Kong Arts Centre (see 7 ◎ Map p70; C3) is a popular venue for dance, theatre and music performances. (香港 藝術中心; ✆2582 0200; www.hkac.org.hk; 2 Harbour Rd, Wan Chai; Ⓜ Wan Chai, exit C)

Street Music Concerts
LIVE MUSIC

Don't miss one of the free outdoor gigs thrown by eclectic musician Kung Chi-sing. One Saturday a month, the musician holds a concert outside the Hong Kong Arts Centre (6.30pm to 9pm). The exciting line-ups have included anything from indie rock, punk and jazz to Cantonese opera and Mozart. It's excellent, professional-quality music performed in an electrifying atmosphere. There's also performances at the Blue House (p73) on the second Thursday of the month (7.30pm to 9.30pm). Check website for dates. (✆2582 0280; www.kungmusic.hk; Wan Chai; admission free)

Wanch LIVE MUSIC

28 Map p70, C3

This place, which derives its name from what everyone calls the district, has live music (mostly rock and folk with the occasional solo guitarist thrown in) seven nights a week from 9pm. Jam night is Monday from 8pm. (☑2861 1621; www.thewanch.hk; 54 Jaffe Rd, Wan Chai; Ⓜ Wan Chai, exit C)

Punchline Comedy Club COMEDY

29 Map p70, E3

A veteran on the scene, the Punchline hosts local and imported acts approximately every third Thursday, Friday and Saturday from 9pm to 11pm. Entry costs around HK$300. Book tickets online or call. (☑2598 1222; www.punchlinecomedy.com/hongkong; 30 Harbour Rd, Tamarind, 2nd fl, Sun Hung Kai Centre, Wan Chai; ⬛18, alight at Wan Chai Sports Ground)

Understand
Hong Kong Festivals

Hong Kong's calendar is littered with colourful festivals celebrating Chinese culture and Western traditions, as well as art, film and music. Here are some of the best events on the Hong Kong entertainment calendar:

Hong Kong Arts Festival (www.hk.artsfestival.org) An extravaganza of music, drama and dance, featuring some of the world's top performers.

Hong Kong Sevens (www.hksevens.com.hk) Rugby teams from all over the world come for three days of lightning-fast, 15-minute matches.

Hong Kong International Film Festival (www.hkiff.org.hk) Film buffs from mainland China and around Asia come to pay homage to Asia's top film festival.

Art Basel Hong Kong (hongkong.artbasel.com) Local and international galleries come to Hong Kong's premier art fair, which takes place at the Hong Kong Convention & Exhibition Centre.

International Dragon Boat Races (www.hkdba.com.hk) Hundreds of teams from the world over compete in Victoria Harbour.

Hong Kong Photo Festival (www.hkphotofest.org) An excellent biennial event that showcases the works of Hong Kong's photographers. Dates change; check the website.

Clockenflap Outdoor Music Festival (www.clockenflap.com) This outdoor indie event in November is the highlight of Hong Kong's live-music calendar.

Shopping

Eslite
BOOKS

You could spend an entire evening inside this swank three-floor Taiwanese bookstore (really – it's open til 2am on weekends), which features a massive collection of English and Chinese books and magazines, a shop selling gorgeous stationary and leather-bound journals, a cafe, a bubble-tea counter, and a huge kids toy and book section (see 34 🔒 Map p70; G3). (☑️3419 6789; 500 Hennessy Rd, Causeway Bay, Hysan Place, 8/f-10/f; ⊙10am-11pm Sun-Thu, to 2am Fri & Sat; Ⓜ️Causeway Bay, exit F2)

Daydream Nation
CLOTHING

Soaring rent has exiled this dreamy nation from its home near Star St to the Hong Kong Arts Centre (see 7 ◉ Map p70; C3). A 'Vogue Talent 2010' brand founded by two of the most creative local designers around (Kay Wong and her brother Jing, who's also a musician), DN is known for its highly wearable fashion and accessories that come with a touch of theatricality. (☑️3741 0758; www.daydream-nation.com; 2 Harbour Rd, 2nd fl, Hong Kong Arts Centre, Wan Chai; ⊙11am-10pm; Ⓜ️Wan Chai, exit C)

Pacific Place
MALL

30 🔒 Map p70, B3

Pacific Place mall has a couple of hundred outlets, dominated by high-end men's and women's fashion and accessories. There's also a **Lane Crawford** (連卡佛; ☑️2118 3398; 88 Queensway, level 1, Pacific Place; ⊙10am-9pm) department store and a **Joyce** (☑️2523 5944; 88 Queensway, Shop 334, 3rd fl, Pacific Place) boutique. (太古廣場; ☑️2844 8988; www.pacificplace.com.hk; 88 Queensway, Admiralty; Ⓜ️Admiralty, exit F)

Kapok
CLOTHING, ACCESSORIES

31 🔒 Map p70, C4

In the hip Star St area, this boutique has a fastidiously edited selection of luxe-cool local and international clothing and accessory labels. Look for their new line of Kapok-label made-in-HK men's shirts, and graphic Mischa handbags by local designer Michelle Lai. The sister boutique is around the corner at 3 Sun St. (☑️2549 9254; www.ka-pok.com; 5 St Francis Yard, Wan Chai; ⊙11am-8pm, to 6pm Sun; Ⓜ️Admiralty, exit F)

Wan Chai Computer Centre
ELECTRONICS

32 🔒 Map p70, D4

This gleaming, beeping warren of tiny shops is a safe bet for anything digital and electronic. (灣仔電腦城; 130-138 Hennessy Rd, 1st fl, Southorn Centre, Wan Chai; ⊙10am-8pm Mon-Sat; Ⓜ️Wan Chai, exit B2)

Kung Fu Supplies
SPORTS

33 🔒 Map p70, E4

If you need to stock up on martial-arts accessories, including uniforms, nun-chakus and safety weapons for practice, or just want to thumb through a decent collection of books and DVDs, this is the place to go. The staff here is very helpful. (功夫用品公司; ☎2891 1912; www.kungfu.com/hk; 188-192 Johnston Rd, Room 6a, 6th fl, Chuen Fung House, Wan Chai; ◷Mon-Sat; ▣6, 6A, 6X)

Hysan Place
MALL

34 🔒 Map p70, G3

This shiny new 17-storey mall is filled with hundreds of ever-trendy Japanese and Korean clothing and beauty brands in a more upscale environment than other local teeny-bopper havens. The 6th-floor Garden of Eden features youth-oriented Asian cosmetics and lingerie labels. (☎2886 7222; www. hp.leegardens.com.hk; 500 Hennessy Rd, Causeway Bay; Ⓜ Causeway Bay, exit F2)

D-mop
CLOTHING, ACCESSORIES

35 🔒 Map p70, H2

Decked out in wood and steel, D-mop has a diverse selection ranging from edgy dressy to chic street, and brands from all over the world. It's one of the few retailers of Y-3 and Nike White Label. (☎2558 0262; www.d-mop.com.hk; 55 Paterson St, Shop B & D, ground fl, Causeway Bay; ◷noon-10pm; Ⓜ Causeway Bay, exit E)

Yiu Fung Store
FOOD

36 🔒 Map p70, G3

Hong Kong's most famous store (c 1960s) for Chinese pickles and preserved fruit features sour plum, liquorice-flavoured lemon, tangerine peel, pickled papaya and dried longan. Just before the Lunar New Year, it's crammed with shoppers. (么鳳; 3

Q **Local Life**

Wan Chai's Markets

The area sandwiched by Queen's Rd East and Johnston Rd in Wan Chai is a lively outdoor bazaar thronged with vendors, shoppers and parked cars. Cross St and the northern section of Stone Nullah Lane features **wet markets** (Map p70, D4; ◷7.30am-7pm) in all their screaming splendour. **Tai Yuen Street** (太原街 (玩具街), *woon gui kaai*), aka 'toy street' to locals, has hawkers selling goldfish, plastic flowers and granny-style underwear, but it's best known for its traditional **toy shops**, where you'll find not only kiddies' playthings, but clockwork tin and other kidult collectibles. Spring Garden Lane and Wan Chai Rd are a treasure trove of shops selling everything from Indian and Southeast Asian spices to funerary offerings and gadgets.

Foo Ming St, Causeway Bay; ◷11am-10pm; Ⓜ Causeway Bay, exit A)

Island Beverley Mall
MALL

37 🔒 Map p70, H3

Crammed into buildings, up escalators and in back lanes are Hong Kong's malls of microshops selling local designer threads, garments from other parts of Asia and a kaleidoscope of kooky accessories. (金百利商場; 1 Great George St, Causeway Bay; Ⓜ Causeway Bay, exit E)

Explore

Hong Kong Island: Aberdeen & the South

This is Hong Kong Island's backyard playground – from the good beaches of Repulse Bay, Deep Water Bay and South Bay to shoppers' paradise Stanley Market and Horizon Plaza, and the excellent Ocean Park amusement park near Aberdeen, which packs in enough entertainment for a whole day.

BRIAN D CRUICKSHANK/GETTY IMAGES ©

The Sights in a Day

Do the half-hour **sampan tour** of the famous Aberdeen Typhoon Shelter, then head to **Horizon Plaza** (p92) in Ap Lei Chau for designer bargains. Spend one to two hours there and have lunch at **Tree Cafe** (p92) inside the plaza. Alternatively, you can spend all morning and most of the afternoon at **Ocean Park** (p89).

Bus it to Stanley and spend the afternoon learning about the colonial history of the southern part of Hong Kong Island. Walk from Stanley Village Road to the **Hong Kong Correctional Services Museum** (p89). After you've had your fill of flogging stands, head back to Stanley to take a 90-minute tour of the historic and beautiful **St Stephen's College** (p89). Make sure you visit the Stanley Military Cemetery next to it. Then indulge in afternoon tea, Hong Kong–style, at **Sei Yik** (p92).

Make your way to **Crown Wine Cellars** (p90) and take a tour of the important WWII bunkers. Have dinner there, accompanied by excellent wine. For a cheaper option, head to Ap Lei Chau and feast on delicious seafood at the **Ap Lei Chau Market Cooked Food Centre** (p90), after checking out the market downstairs.

For a local's day in the southern beaches, see p86.

 Local Life

Beach-Hopping on Island South (p86)

 Best of Hong Kong

Beaches

South Bay (p87)

Middle Bay (p87)

St Stephen's Beach (p87)

Eating

Ap Lei Chau Market Cooked Food Centre (p90)

Spices Restaurant (p87)

Jumbo Kingdom Floating Restaurant (p91)

Getting There

🚌 **Bus** Stanley, Repulse Bay & Deep Water Bay: buses 6A, 6X, 260 from below Exchange Sq (Central); buses 73, 973 from Aberdeen.

🚌 **Bus** Aberdeen: buses 73 and 973 from Stanley.

🚌 **Bus** Ap Lei Chau: bus 90 from Admiralty bus terminus; by commuter boat from Aberdeen Promenade.

Local Life
Beach-Hopping on Island South

Beach-hopping along the Island's southern coastline is fun and convenient. Lots of beaches have showers and changing facilities, and most have other sights and restaurants in the vicinity. In the summer the waters around Stanley and Repulse Bay teem with bioluminescent algae. Go after sundown to swim with fireflies.

❶ Deep Water Bay

Start from the westernmost Deep Water Bay, a quiet little inlet with a beach flanked by shade trees. Though not as famous as its neighbour Repulse Bay, it's less crowded and its barbecue pits are a real draw for locals – a dip here, especially in late afternoon, is sometimes accompanied by the aromas of grilled meat.

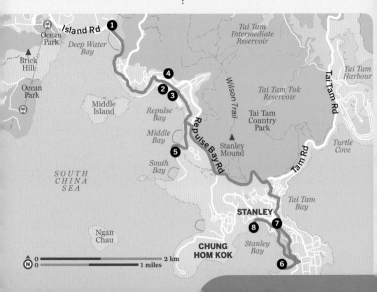

❷ Repulse Bay

From Deep Water Bay, take the scenic Seaview Promenade 2km to Repulse Bay, and be greeted by the sight of families and joggers going about their business. The long beach with tawny sand at Repulse Bay is packed almost all the time in summer. The water is murky, but it's good for people-watching.

❸ Around Repulse Bay

The hills here are strewn with luxury residences, including a wavy pastel building with a square hole in the middle (p90), apparently a feature related to feng shui. At the beach's southeast end there's an assembly of deities and figures, as well as **Longevity Bridge** (長壽橋) – crossing the bridge is supposed to add three days to your life.

❹ Spices Restaurant

Spices (香辣軒; ☎ 2292 2821; www.therepulsebay.com; 109 Repulse Bay Rd, Repulse Bay; meals from HK$200; ⏰ noon-2.30pm & 6.30-10.30pm Mon-Fri, 11.30am-10.30pm Sat & Sat; 🚌 6, 6A, 6X, 260), with its airy, colonial-style tropical interiors, is an ideal place for tea or a sundowner after a day at the beach. Sit on the terrace and enjoy palatable Asian selections such as curries and satays. Don't miss the homemade coconut ice cream!

❺ Middle Bay & South Bay

These attractive beaches are respectively 1km and 2km to the south of Repulse Bay. Middle Bay is popular with gay beachgoers, while French expats are drawn to South Bay. Swimming here on summer nights, you'll see specks of algae glowing like stars in the water.

❻ St Stephen's Beach

This hidden spot south of Stanley village is cleaner than Stanley Main Beach, and there are windsurfing boards and kayaks for hire. Take the bus to Stanley then walk south along Wong Ma Kok Rd. Turn right into Wong Ma Kok Path, then turn south and go past the boathouse to the **beach** (🚌 6A, 14).

❼ Stanley Market

In Stanley village the busy and labyrinthine **market** (赤柱市集; Stanley Village Rd; ⏰ 9am-6pm; 🚌 6, 6A, 6X or 260) has reasonably priced casual clothes (including large sizes and children's wear), linens, bric-a-brac and formulaic art.

❽ Murray House

Relocated from Central, **Murray House** (美利樓; Stanley Bay; 🚌 6, 6A, 6X, 260) (c 1844) is a three-storey classical building with breezy, wrap-around verandahs and a tiled roof with Chinese characteristics common in colonial architecture of that era.

THE PEAK

Pok Fu Lam Village 2

SIU SAI WAN

CHAI WAN

Tai Tam Rd

Pottinger Peak (312m)

Big Wave Bay Rd

Hong Kong Trail

SHEK O

9

11

Shek O Rd

D'Aguilar Peak (323m)

Shek O Country Park

Shek O Peak (284m)

Hong Kong Trail

Tai Tam Rd

Tai Tam Harbour

Tai Tam Country Park

Mt Butler (436m)

Jardine's Lookout

Hong Kong Trail

Tai Tam Reservoir

Tai Tam Tuk Reservoir

Hong Kong Correctional Services

Tai Tam Rd

St Stephen's College

Museum 4

STANLEY

15 13 10 3

Stanley Bay

Stubbs Rd

Violet Hill (433m)

Tai Tam Intermediate Reservoir

Tai Tam Country Park

Stanley Mound (386m)

Wilson Trail

Crown Wine Cellars

12

Repulse Bay Rd

CHUNG HOM KOK

Mt Nicholson (430m)

Ocean Park

Deep Water Bay

Repulse Bay

South Bay

Middle Island

Ngan Chau

Aberdeen Country Park

Aberdeen Lower Reservoir

WONG CHUK HANG

1

5

Brick Hill

Ocean Park

Sham Wan

8

ABERDEEN

6 7

AP LEI CHAU

14

Aberdeen Channel

Ap Lei Pai

SOUTH CHINA SEA

Sampan Tours

East Lamma Channel

MO TAT WAN

Lamma

For reviews see

Sights	p89
Eating	p90
Shopping	p92

4 km

2 miles

N

Sights

Ocean Park

AMUSEMENT PARK

1 ◎ Map p88, B2

It may have to compete with the natural crowd-pulling powers of Disneyland on Lantau Island, but for many Ocean Park remains the top theme park in Hong Kong. The park's constant expansion and addition of new rides and thrills, as well as the presence of four giant pandas plus two very cute, rare red pandas – all gifts from the mainland – has kept this a must-visit for families. (☑3923 2323; www.oceanpark.com.hk; Ocean Park Rd; adult/child 3-11yr HK\$320/160; ☺10am-7.30pm; ♿; ☐629 from Admiralty, ☐973 from Tsim Sha Tsui, ☐6A, 6X, 70, 75 from Central, ☐72, 72A, 92 from Causeway Bay)

Pok Fu Lam Village

VILLAGE

2 ◎ Map p88, A1

Located on a sloping hillside, Pok Fu Lam Village, a settlement full of shacks and makeshift huts, is quite a contrast to the condos behind. You can catch a glimpse of the Hong Kong of yesteryear when refugees from China built their temporary-turned-permanent homes here. There's a 200-year-old pagoda on the northern side of the village, and a spectacular fire dragon dance takes place here during the Mid-Autumn Festival. (薄扶林村; www.pokfulamvillage.org; ☐7, 40, 40M, 90B, 91)

Hong Kong Correctional Services Museum

MUSEUM

3 ◎ Map p88, D4

Mock cells, gallows and flogging stands are the gruesome draws at this museum, about 500m southeast of Stanley Village Rd, which traces the history of jails, prisons and other forms of incarceration in Hong Kong. (香港懲教博物館; ☑2147 3199; www.csd.gov.hk/emuseum; 45 Tung Tau Wan Rd; admission free; ☺10am-5pm Tue-Sun; ☐6, 6A, 6X, 260)

St Stephen's College

HISTORIC SITE

4 ◎ Map p88, D4

WWII history buffs can visit the beautiful campus of St Stephen's College which sits right next to Stanley Military

---

Understand
The Murray Puzzle

Murray House (p87) was relocated to Stanley in 2001 to make room for the Bank of China Building in Central. The Grade 1 heritage building was dismantled piece by piece, and all 4000 numbered pieces painstakingly reassembled at its new waterfront home. However, after the colossus was put back together again, six columns were left over – you'll see the Ionic columns standing rather forlornly off to the left along the waterfront promenade. Note, too, some of the numbers still visible on the building blocks to the right of the entrance.

Understand
Hole in the Soul

Repulse Bay is surrounded by swanky high-rise apartment blocks. Among them is a giant pink, blue and yellow wavy structure with a huge square hole in the middle. Apparently, this design feature was added on the advice of a feng shui expert. 'Chi', or energy flowing over mountains, is sometimes called a 'mountain dragon', and its course is called a 'dragon's vein'. Not all mountains have dragon's veins, but apparently this one does. And if it wasn't for the hole, the building would block the downward flow of this precious energy to the water, which would bring bad luck to the entire neighbourhood.

Cemetery. Founded in 1903, the school was turned into an emergency military hospital on the eve of the Japanese invasion of Hong Kong in 1941 and became an internment camp after the city fell. The 1½-hour guided tour by students takes you to eight sites in the campus. (聖士提反書院文物徑; ☑2813 0360; www.ssc.edu.hk/ssctrail/eng; 22 Tung Tau Wan Rd; admission free; ☐6, 6A, 6X, 260)

Crown Wine Cellars HISTORIC SITE

5 ◉ Map p88, C2

The WWII bunkers on the hill have been transformed into a top-notch wine cellar, with a colonial-style glasshouse restaurant surrounded by towering trees. You can tour the site and have a meal there by subscribing to the one-time 'silver' membership free of charge. (☑2580 6287; www.crownwinecellars.com; 18 Deep Water Bay Dr, Shouson Hill; ☐minibus 5 from Lockhart Rd, behind Sogo dept store in Causeway Bay)

Sampan Tours BOAT TRIPS

6 ◉ Map p88, A2

Sampan tours are a fun way to see parts of the island's south coast, and you can easily find sampan operators milling around the eastern end of the Aberdeen Promenade. Usually they charge around HK$68 per person for a 30-minute ride (about HK$120 to Sok Kwu Wan and HK$150 to Yung Shue Wan on Lamma). (Aberdeen Promenade; ☐70 to Aberdeen)

Eating

Ap Lei Chau Market
Cooked Food Centre DAI PAI DONG $

7 ✕ Map p88, A2

Sharing a building with a market, six *dai pai dong* (food stall) operators cook up a storm in sleepy Ap Lei Chau. **Pak Kee** (栢記; ☑2555 2984; ◷dinner) and **Chu Kee** (珠記; ☑2555 2052; ◷dinner) both offer tasty seafood dishes in the HK$40 to HK$60 range. You can also buy seafood from the wet market downstairs and pay them to cook it for you the way you want. (鴨利洲市政大廈; 8 Hung Shing St, 1st fl, Ap Lei Chau Municipal Services Bldg; meals from HK$40; ☐minibus 36X from Lee Garden Rd, Causeway Bay)

FUMIO OKADA/ROBERT HARDING ©

Repulse Bay

Jumbo Kingdom Floating Restaurant CANTONESE $$

8 Map p88, B2

A three-story floating extravaganza moored in Aberdeen Harbour, the Jumbo looks like Běijīng's Imperial Palace crossbred with Macau's Casino Lisboa – a spectacle so kitsch it's fun. Celebrity visitors have included everyone from Queen Elizabeth to Tom Cruise to Chow Yun Fat. Eschew the overpriced Dragon Court on the 2nd floor and head to the 3rd floor for dim sum. (珍寶海鮮舫; ☑2553 9111; www. jumbo.com.hk; Shum Wan Pier Dr, Wong Chuk Hang; meals from HK$120; ⏰11am-11.30pm Mon-Sat, from 9am Sun; ☐90 from Central)

Black Sheep INTERNATIONAL $$

9 Map p88, E3

With batik tablecloths, a plant-filled patio and a hand-written chalkboard menu, this back-alley bistro exudes hippie vibes. Pizzas and seafood are favourites, and there's always a veggie option. (黑羊餐廳; ☑2809 2021; 330 Shek O Village; meals from HK$180; ⏰6-9pm Mon-Fri, noon-9pm Sat & Sun; ✏; ☐9 from Shau Kei Wan MTR station, exit A3)

Toby Inn CANTONESE $

10 Map p88, D3

This modest eatery is the neighbourhood restaurant of Stanley, with elderly people dropping in for dim sum at the crack of dawn, dragon boaters stopping by for seafood after practice, and families coming in for simple dishes throughout the day. (赤柱酒家; ☎2813 2880; U1-U2, 126 Stanley Main St; meals HK$80-150; ☉5.30am-10.30pm; ☒6, 6A, 6X or 260)

Happy Garden THAI $

11 Map p88, E3

This humble mum-and-dad operation makes everyone happy with fresh seafood, authentic Thai fare and decent prices. Upstairs, the terrace offers some views of the ocean. The restaurant is in front of the car park by the beach. (石澳樂園; ☎2809 4165; 786 Shek O Village; lunch/dinner from HK$50/80; ☉11.30am-11pm; ☒9 from Shau Kei Wan MTR station, exit A3)

Verandah INTERNATIONAL $$$

12 Map p88, C2

A meal in the grand Verandah, run by the prestigious Peninsula, is a special occasion indeed. The large restaurant features a recently restored and refurbished interior that is literally dripping with colonial nostalgia, what with the grand piano at the entrance, the wooden fans dangling from the ceiling, and the marble staircases with wooden banisters. (露台餐廳; ☎2292 2822; www.therepulsebay.com; 109 Repulse Bay Rd, 1st fl, the Repulse Bay; meals from HK$400; ☉noon-2.30pm, 3-5.30pm & 7-10.30pm, brunch 11am-2.30pm Sun; ☒6, 6A, 6X, 260)

Sei Yik CANTONESE, DAI PAI DONG $

13 Map p88, D3

Weekenders flock to this small tin-roofed *dai pai dong*, right opposite the Stanley Municipal Building, for its fluffy Hong Kong–style French toast with *kaya* (coconut jam) spread. No English signage; look for the long queue of pilgrims and the piles of fruits that hide the entrance. (泗益; ☎2813 0503; 2 Stanley Market St; meals from HK$30; ☉6am-7pm Wed-Mon)

Shopping

Horizon Plaza OUTLETS

14 🔒 Map p88, A2

Tucked away on the southern coast of Ap Lei Chau, this enormous outlet, in a converted factory building, boasts more than 150 shops over 28 storeys. Most locals come here to buy furniture, but you'll also find Alexander McQueens on offer and Jimmy Choos at knock-down prices. (新海怡廣場; 2 Lee Wing St, Ap Lei Chau, Aberdeen; ☉10am-7pm; ☒90 from Exchange Sq in Central)

Take a Break The airy **Tree Cafe** (Map p88, A2; ☎2870 1582; www.tree.com.hk/cafe; 2 Lee Wing St, 28/F, Horizon Plaza, Ap Lei Chau; meals from HK$60; ☉10.30am-7pm; ♿; ☒90 from Central) offers solid sandwiches (from HK$45) and coffee.

G.O.D. CLOTHING, HOUSEWARES

15 🔒 Map p88, D3

One of the coolest born-in-Hong Kong shops around, G.O.D. does irreverent takes on classic Hong Kong iconography. (Goods of Desire; ☎2673 0071; www.god.co.hk; 22-23 Stanley Rd, Stanley, Shop 105, Stanley Plaza; ☉10.30am-8pm; ☒6, 6A, 6X, 260)

Understand

Fishing Culture in Aberdeen

The main attraction of fishing port Aberdeen is the typhoon shelter (featured in the second *Lara Croft: Tomb Raider* movie) it shares with sleepy Ap Lei Chau, where the sampans of the boat-dwelling Tanka, a group that arrived in Hong Kong before the 10th century, used to be moored. Sometimes referred to as 'sea gypsies' by the British, the Tankas are believed to be descendants of certain ethnic minorities of southern China.

In 1961 the boat-dwelling population here stood at 28,000; now only a few hundred remain. While Lara Croft saw entire families going about their idyllic lives on a boat, you'll see motorised junks next to luxury yachts, and rusty shipyards alongside gleaming high-rises. In downtown Aberdeen dry seafood stalls and mini-malls stand cheek by jowl.

People of the Water

The majority of inhabitants in Aberdeen and Ap Lei Chau are descendants of Tanka fishermen, and still see themselves as 'people of the water' (水上人; *sui seung yan*) and understand Tanka dialect. Each year this identity is flaunted with fanfare at dragon-boat races held throughout the territory. On weekday evenings you may spot teams practising under the moon in the typhoon shelter, or chilling out in the Ap Lei Chau Market Cooked Food Centre after practice.

Dragon Boat

Hong Kong is the home of modern dragon-boat racing, an activity that originated 2000 years ago as a ritual for worshipping water deities. The city has the most teams (about 400) and the most races (over 20 per year) in the world, per square metre. It's a sport zealously embraced by all walks of life. Come racing season, even pasty-faced office workers will take up a paddle. The most spectacular events during the racing season (March to October) are the fishermen's races. You'll see junks moored in the harbour and decked out with flags, and people casting paper offerings into the water. **Dragon Boat Association** (www.hkdba.com.hk) and **Hong Kong Tourist Board** (www.discoverhongkong.com) have listings of major events.

Explore

Kowloon: Tsim Sha Tsui

Tsim Sha Tsui (TST), meaning 'sharp sandy point', is a vibrant district occupying the southern tip of the Kowloon Peninsula. Though best known for its shopping and dining, TST is also thick with museums and performance spaces. And with a population comprising Chinese, Indians, Filipinos, Nepalese, Africans and Europeans, it's Hong Kong's most cosmopolitan corner.

The Sights in a Day

Spend two hours at the **Museum of History** (p99), then stroll the scenic **Tsim Sha Tsui East Promenade** (p96) to the Star Ferry Concourse, stopping to see any or all of the following along the way: **Middle Road Children's Playground** (p101), **Hong Kong Museum of Art** (p97), the **Clock Tower** (p97). Have Indian vegetarian lunch in between sights at **Woodlands** (p103).

Spend some time exploring Tsim Sha Tsui's unique heritage – the **Former Marine Police Headquarters** (p100), **Fook Tak Ancient Temple** (p100), **Kowloon Mosque** (p102), **St Andrew's Anglican Church** (p99), **Former Kowloon British School** (p101) – ending with afternoon tea at the **Peninsula Hong Kong** (p102) or samosas and lassi at **Chungking Mansions** (p100). Then head to the **Ocean Terminal** (p111) for retail therapy.

Have dinner at **Great Beef Hot Pot** (p104), followed by cocktails at **Butler** (p106).

 Top Sights

Tsim Sha Tsui East Promenade (p96)

Best of Hong Kong

Eating
Gaddi's (p103)

Great Beef Hot Pot (p104)

Woodlands (p103)

Spring Deer (p104)

Din Tai Fung (p104)

Yè Shanghai (p104)

Typhoon Shelter Hing Kee Restaurant (p104)

Museums
Hong Kong Museum of History (p99)

Hong Kong Museum of Art (p97)

June 4th Museum (p101)

Getting There

Ⓜ **Metro** Tsim Sha Tsui and Jordan stations (Tsuen Wan line); East Tsim Sha Tsui station (West Rail line).

⚓ **Star Ferry** Western end of Salisbury Rd.

⚓ **Macau Ferries** The China Ferry Terminal (p141) is on Canton Rd.

Top Sights
Tsim Sha Tsui East Promenade

The resplendent views of Victoria Harbour make
this walkway one of the best strolls in Hong
Kong. Go during the day to take photos, visit the
museums along the way and watch watercraft,
families, lovers and tourists going about their
business. After sundown, on your way to dinner
or the Star Ferry, revisit the views, now magically
transformed with skyscrapers decked out in their
neon robes.

👁 Map p98, D4

尖沙嘴東部海濱花園

Salisbury Rd, Tsim Sha
Tsui

Ⓜ Tsim Sha Tsui, exit E

Avenue of the Stars

Don't Miss

Clock Tower

The old Kowloon–Canton Railway Clock Tower (c 1915), in red brick and granite, is a landmark of the age of steam. The clocks began ticking on 22 March 1921 and haven't stopped since, except during the Japanese occupation.

Avenue of the Stars

Further north is Hong Kong's lacklustre tribute (星光大道) to its once-brilliant film industry. The highlight is a 2.5m-tall bronze statue of kung-fu icon Bruce Lee.

Hong Kong Museum of Art

This excellent **museum** (香港藝術館; ☎2721 0116; http://hk.art.museum; 10 Salisbury Rd, Tsim Sha Tsui; adult/concession HK$10/5, Wed free; ⏰10am-6pm Mon-Fri, to 7pm Sat & Sun) has seven galleries exhibiting Chinese antiquities and fine art, historical pictures and contemporary Hong Kong art; it also hosts temporary international exhibitions. Free English tours 11am Tuesday to Sunday.

Space Museum & Science Museum

The **Space Museum** (香港太空館; ☎2721 0226; www.lcsd.gov.hk; 10 Salisbury Rd, Tsim Sha Tsui; adult/concession HK$10/5, shows HK$24/12, Wed free; ⏰1-9pm Mon & Wed-Fri, 10am-9pm Sat & Sun; 🖐) has 'sky shows', Omnimax films and a virtual paraglider. The giftshop sells dehydrated ice cream. Three storeys of action-packed displays at the **Science Museum** (香港科學館; ☎2732 3232; http://hk.science. museum; 2 Science Museum Rd, Tsim Sha Tsui; adult/concession HK$25/12.50, Wed free; ⏰10am-7pm Mon-Wed & Fri, to 9pm Sat & Sun; 🖐) are a big attraction for youngsters.

☑ Top Tips

▶ Stairs near the Clock Tower lead to an elevated observation area.

▶ Stairs and a lift just past Avenue of the Stars lead to Tsim Sha Tsui East Podium Garden and Middle Road Children's Playground (p101).

▶ From Avenue of the Stars you can watch the **Symphony of Lights** (⏰8-8.20pm), the world's largest permanent laser light show, projected from atop 40 skyscrapers.

✗ Take a Break

Deck 'N Beer (Map p98, D4; ☎2723 9227; Tsim Sha Tsui East Promenade; ⏰3-11pm Mon-Thu, to 1am Fri & Sat, 1-11pm Sun; Ⓜ Tsim Sha Tsui) at the Avenue of the Stars offers open frontage and decent beer. The classy **InterContinental Lobby Lounge** (p106) has upmarket snacks and drinks.

For reviews see

◉ Top Sights	p96
◎ Sights	p99
⊗ Eating	p103
⊗ Drinking	p106
✪ Entertainment	p109
🛈 Shopping	p110

0 ————— 200 m
0 ————— 0.1 miles

Sights

Hong Kong Museum of History
MUSEUM

1 Map p98, E1

For a whistle-stop overview of the territory's archaeology, ethnography, and natural and local history, this museum is well worth a visit, not only to learn more about the subject but also to understand how Hong Kong presents its stories to the world.

'The Hong Kong Story' takes visitors on a fascinating walk through the territory's past via eight galleries, starting with the natural environment and prehistoric Hong Kong – about 6000 years ago, give or take a lunar year – and ending with the territory's return to China in 1997. You'll encounter replicas of village dwellings; traditional Chinese costumes and beds; a re-creation of an entire arcaded street in Central from 1881, including an old Chinese medicine shop; a tram from 1913; and film footage of WWII, including recent interviews with Chinese and foreigners taken prisoner by the Japanese.

Free guided tours of the museum are available in English at 11am. (香港歷史博物館; ☑ 2724 9042; http://hk.history.museum; 100 Chatham Rd South, Tsim Sha Tsui; adult/concession HK$10/5, Wed free; ☉10am-6pm Mon & Wed-Sat, to 7pm Sun; 👬; Ⓜ Tsim Sha Tsui, exit B2)

Take a Break Grab some Indonesian snacks from **Indonesia Restaurant** (Map p98, D2; 印尼餐廳; 66 Granville Rd; meals HK$80-200; ☉noon-3pm & 5-11pm

Mon-Fri, noon-11pm Sat & Sun; Ⓜ Tsim Sha Tsui, exit B1), across the road.

St Andrew's Anglican Church
CHURCH

2 Map p98, C1

Sitting atop a knoll, next to the Former Kowloon British School, is a charming building in English Gothic style that houses Kowloon's oldest Protestant church. St Andrew's was built in 1905 in granite and red brick to serve Kowloon's Protestant population; it was turned into a Shinto shrine during the Japanese occupation. Nearby you'll see the handsome former vicarage with columned balconies (c 1909). Enter from the eastern side of Nathan Rd via steps or a slope. (聖安德烈堂; ☑ 2367 1478; www.standrews.org.hk; 138 Nathan Rd, Tsim Sha Tsui; ☉7.30am-10.30pm, church 8.30am-5.30pm; Ⓜ Tsim Sha Tsui, exit B1)

☑ Top Tip

Hong Kong Museums Pass

The Hong Kong Museums Pass allows multiple entries to six of Hong Kong's museums: the Science Museum, Hong Kong Museum of History, Hong Kong Museum of Art, Space Museum (excluding the Space Theatre), Hong Kong Heritage Museum and Hong Kong Museum of Coastal Defence. It's available from any Hong Kong Tourism Board (HKTB) outlet and the participating museums.

Fook Tak Ancient Temple

TEMPLE

3 Map p98, B3

Tsim Sha Tsui's only temple is a smoke-filled hole in the wall with a hot tin roof. Little is known about its ancestry except that it was built as a shrine in the Qing dynasty and renovated in 1900. Before WWII, worshippers of its Earth God were coolies from nearby Kowloon Wharf, where the **Ocean Terminal** (www.oceanterminal.com.hk; Salisbury Rd, Tsim Sha Tsui; ☺10am-9pm; ✿Star Ferry, MEast Tsim Sha Tsui, exit J) now stands. Today most incense offerers are octogenarians – the temple specialises in longevity. (福德古廟; 30 Haiphong Rd, Tsim Sha Tsui; ☺6am-8pm; MTsim Sha Tsui, exit C2)

Local Life
Learn Taichi

Let a spritely master show you how to 'spread your wings like a stork' and 'wave hands like clouds' against the views of Victoria Harbour in front of the Hong Kong Museum of Art. Taichi, or shadow boxing, is supposed to give you a sharper mind and a fitter heart. The **lesson** (☎Pandora 9415 5678, William 9554 6928; Tsim Sha Tsui East Promenade; taichi HK$50; ☺7.30-9am Mon, Wed & Fri; MTsim Sha Tsui, exit J) is offered by instructors who used to teach for the Hong Kong Tourism Board. Preregistration not required – just show up.

Take a Break Tak Fat Beef Balls (Map p98, B2; 德發牛肉丸; Haiphong Rd, Haiphong Rd Temporary Market, Tsim Sha Tsui; beef ball noodles HK$26; ☺9am-8pm; MTsim Sha Tsui, exit A1), in Haiphong Road Temporary Market next door, has cheap noodles with beef balls and Hong Kong–style milk tea.

Chungking Mansions

BUILDING

4 Map p98, C3

Say 'budget accommodation' and 'Hong Kong' in one breath and everyone thinks of Chungking Mansions. This huge, ramshackle high-rise caters to virtually all needs – from finding a bed and a curry lunch to changing your Burmese kyat and getting your hair cut. The building's infamy is fuelled by tales both tall and true of conflagrations and crimes. Everyone should come here once. (重慶大廈, CKM; 36-44 Nathan Rd, Tsim Sha Tsui; admission free; MTsim Sha Tsui, exit D1)

Former Marine Police Headquarters

HISTORIC BUILDING

5 Map p98, B4

Built in 1884, this gorgeous Victorian complex is one of Hong Kong's four oldest government buildings. It was used continuously by the Hong Kong Marine Police except during WWII when the Japanese navy took over. The complex is now a nakedly commercial property called 'Heritage 1881'. Some of the old structures are still here, including stables, pigeon houses and a bomb shelter.

Why 1881? Because '4' has a similar pronunciation to 'death' in Chinese, and the developer was superstitious. (前水警總部; 2926 8000, tour reservation 2926 1881; www.1881heritage.com; 2A Canton Rd, Tsim Sha Tsui; admission free; ☉10am-10pm; 🚢Star Ferry, Ⓜ East Tsim Sha Tsui, exit L6)

June 4th Museum
MUSEUM

6 ◉ Map p98, D1

The world's first permanent museum dedicated to the 1989 pro-democracy protests in Běijīng's Tiān'ānmén Square. The 800 sq ft space has artefacts, photographs, books and microfilm related to the incident including casings of bullets supposedly fired by the People's Liberation Army (PLA) and T-shirts signed by the Běijīng student leaders such as Wang Dan. A copy of the Goddess of Democracy statue built by the students stands at the heart of the museum. (六四紀念館; 2782 6111; www.64museum.org; 3 Austin Ave, 5th fl, Foo Hoo Centre, Tsim Sha Tsui; adult/concession HK$10/5; ☉10am-6pm Mon, Wed-Fri, to 7pm Sat & Sun; Ⓜ Jordan, exit D)

Former Kowloon British School
HISTORIC BUILDING

7 ◉ Map p98, C1

The oldest surviving school building for expat children is a listed Victorian-style structure that now houses the **Antiquities and Monuments Office** (古物古蹟辦事處). Established in 1902, it was subsequently modified to incorporate breezy verandahs and

Chungking Mansions

high ceilings, prompted possibly by the fainting spells suffered by its young occupants. (前九龍英童學校; www.amo.gov.hk; 136 Nathan Rd, Tsim Sha Tsui; Ⓜ Tsim Sha Tsui, exit B1)

Take a Break Enjoy beer and German sausages at **King Ludwig Beer Hall** (Map p98, D4; 2369 8328; www.kingparrot.com; 32 Salisbury Rd, Tsim Sha Tsui; ☉noon-1am Sun-Thu, to 2am Fri & Sat; Ⓜ East Tsim Sha Tsui, exit K), at the foot of the steps leading to the park.

Middle Road Children's Playground
PARK

8 ◉ Map p98, D4

Accessible via a sweep of stairs from Chatham Rd South, this hidden gem atop the East Tsim Sha Tsui MTR station has play facilities, shaded seating and views of the waterfront. On weekdays it's the quiet backyard playground of the residents nearby, but on weekends it's filled with children and picnickers of as many ethnicities as there are ways to go down a slide (if you're eight). (中間道兒童遊樂場; Middle Rd, Tsim Sha Tsui; ⏰7am-11pm; 🚻; Ⓜ East Tsim Sha Tsui, exit K)

Peninsula Hong Kong

HISTORIC BUILDING

9 ◎ Map p98, C4

The Peninsula (c 1928), in a throne-like building, is one of the world's great hotels. Though it was once called 'the finest hotel east of Suez', the Pen was in fact one of several prestigious hotels across Asia, lining up with (but not behind) the likes of the Raffles in Singapore and the Cathay (now the Peace) in Shànghǎi. Taking afternoon tea here is a wonderful experience – dress neatly and be prepared to queue for a table. (香港半島酒店; www.peninsula.com; cnr Salisbury & Nathan Rds, Tsim Sha Tsui; Ⓜ East Tsim Sha Tsui, exit L3)

Kowloon Mosque & Islamic Centre

MOSQUE

10 ◎ Map p98, C2

This structure, with its dome and carved marble, is Hong Kong's largest mosque. It serves the territory's 70,000-odd Muslims, more than half of whom are Chinese, and accommodates up to 3000 worshippers. The mosque was originally established to serve the Indian Muslim troops of the British army who were stationed at what is now Kowloon Park. Muslims are welcome to attend services, but non-Muslims should ask permission to enter. Remember to remove your footwear. (九龍清真寺; 📞2724 0095; http://kowloonmosque.com; 105 Nathan Rd, Tsim Sha Tsui; ⏰5am-10pm; Ⓜ Tsim Sha Tsui, exit C2)

Take a Break Unwind over reasonably priced meze and a shisha at **Ziafat** (Map p98, C3; 📞2312 1015; 81 Nathan Rd, 6th fl, Harilela Mansion, Tsim Sha Tsui; meals HK$80-200; ⏰noon-midnight; 🍴; Ⓜ Tsim Sha Tsui, exit R).

Kowloon Park

PARK

11 ◎ Map p98, B2

Built on the site of a barracks for Indian soldiers in the colonial army, Kowloon Park is an oasis of greenery and a refreshing escape from the hustle and bustle of Tsim Sha Tsui. Pathways and walls criss-cross the grass, birds hop around in cages, and ancient banyan trees dot the landscape. In the morning the older set practise taichi amid the serene surrounds, and on Sunday afternoon Kung Fu Corner stages martial arts displays. (九龍公園; www.lcsd.gov.hk; Nathan & Austin Rds, Tsim Sha Tsui; ⏰6am-midnight; 🚻; Ⓜ Tsim Sha Tsui, exit C2)

RICHARD I'ANSON/GETTY IMAGES ©

Afternoon tea, Peninsula Hong Kong

Eating

Gaddi's
FRENCH $$$

12 Map p98, C4

Gaddi's, which opened just after WWII, was the kind of place where wealthy families went to celebrate special occasions. Today the classical decor may be a tad stuffy, the live Filipino band gratuitous, but the food – traditional French with contemporary touches – is without a doubt still among the best in town. (📞2696 6763; www.peninsula.com/Hong_Kong; 19-21 Salisbury Rd, 1st fl, the Peninsula, Tsim Sha Tsui; set lunch/dinner HK$500/2000; ⏰noon-2.30pm & 7-10.30pm; Ⓜ Tsim Sha Tsui, exit E)

Woodlands
INDIAN, VEGETARIAN $

13 Map p98, D3

Located above a department store, good old Woodlands offers excellent-value Indian vegetarian food to compatriots and the odd local. Dithering gluttons should order the *thali* meal, which is served on a round metal plate with 10 tiny dishes, a dessert and bread. (活蘭印度素食; 📞2369 3718; 62 Mody Rd, upper ground fl, 16 & 17 Wing On Plaza, Tsim Sha Tsui; meals HK$70-180; ⏰noon-3.30pm & 6.30-10.30pm; 🍴♿; Ⓜ East Tsim Sha Tsui, exit P1)

Spring Deer
NORTHERN CHINESE **$$**

14 🍴 Map p98, D3

Hong Kong's most authentic Northern-style roasted lamb is served here. Yet better known is the Peking duck, which is very good. That said, the service can be about as welcoming as a Běijīng winter, c 1967. Booking is essential. (鹿鳴春飯店; 📞2366 4012; 42 Mody Rd, 1st fl, Tsim Sha Tsui; meals HK$80-500; 🕐noon-3pm & 6-11pm; Ⓜ East Tsim Sha Tsui, exit N2)

Yè Shanghai
SHANGHAINESE, DIM SUM **$$**

15 🍴 Map p98, B4

The name means 'Shànghǎi Nights'. Dark woods and subtle lighting inspired by 1920s Shànghǎi fill the air with romance. The modern Shanghainese dishes are also exquisite. The only exception to this Jiāngnán harmony is the Cantonese dim sum being served at lunch, though that too is wonderful. Sophisticated Yè Shanghai has one Michelin star. (夜上海; 📞2376 3322; www.elite-concepts.com; Canton Rd, 6th fl, Marco Polo Hotel, Harbour City, Tsim Sha Tsui; meals HK$400-800; 🕐11.30am-2.30pm & 6-10.30pm; ♿; Ⓜ Tsim Sha Tsui, exit C2)

Din Tai Fung
TAIWANESE, NOODLES **$$**

16 🍴 Map p98, B3

Whether it's comfort food or a carb fix you're craving, the juicy Shanghai dumplings and hearty Northern-style noodles at this Taiwanese chain will do the trick. Queues are the norm and it doesn't take reservations, but service is excellent. DTF has one Michelin star. (鼎泰豐; 📞2730 6928; www.dintaifung.com.hk; 30 Canton Rd, Shop 130, 3rd fl, Silvercord, Tsim Sha Tsui; meals HK$120-300; 🕐11.30am-10.30pm; ♿; Ⓜ Tsim Sha Tsui, exit C1)

Typhoon Shelter Hing Kee Restaurant
CANTONESE **$$**

17 🍴 Map p98, C1

This celebrity haunt is run by a feisty fisherman's daughter who's known for her brilliant dishes prepared the way they were on sampans. The signature crabs smothered in a mountain of fried garlic are a wonder to taste and behold. The service can be a little edgy. Be sure you know the price of every dish before you order. (避風塘興記; 📞2722 0022; 180 Nathan Rd, 1st fl Bowa House, Tsim Sha Tsui; meals HK$380-1200; 🕐6pm-5am; Ⓜ Jordan, exit D)

Great Beef Hot Pot
HOTPOT **$$**

18 🍴 Map p98, D2

Indecisive gluttons will scream at the mind-blowing hotpot choices here – 200 ingredients (the majority fresh or homemade; HK$25 to HK$270), 20 kinds of broth (from clam soup to fancy herbal concoctions; HK$68 to HK$468), and an embarrassment of condiments (all-you-can-dip)! There's no escaping the menu either, the lights are too bright! Now onto the sashimi options... Booking essential. (禾牛薈火煱館; 📞3997 3369; 48 Cameron

Understand
TST, Breeze for the Feet

The crowds and the traffic might obscure it, but Tsim Sha Tsui (TST) is one of the most walkable urban areas in Hong Kong. Architect Freddie Hai once put a ruler on the area's footpaths and found most to be 250m to 300m in length. Metro stations have a catchment radius of 500m, the rough equivalent of an eight-minute stroll. At half the length, streets in TST take only four minutes to walk.

What's more, linking most of TST's meandering avenues are T-junctions (where one road joins another at right angles but does not cross it). The very layout of the T-junction creates a sense of neighbourly enclosure while dangling the promise of fresh horizons at every corner. So reaching Canton Rd from Peking Rd, would it be right to the Macau Ferry Terminal or left to the Space Museum? Compare this to the sprawling, criss-crossing grid that is Yau Ma Tei – a fascinating area buzzing with life, which could also alienate or disorient if you're new to it.

Good old Nathan Rd is never more than four blocks away, no matter where you're in TST. Beginning just shy of the harbour, Kowloon's earliest strip of asphalt runs past Yau Ma Tei to end in Mong Kok, offering the reassurance of a linear narrative in a labyrinthine plot, and a choice of many, many endings.

Rd, 1st & 2nd fl, China Insurance Bldg, Tsim Sha Tsui; meals HK$350-600; �is5.30pm-2am; M Tsim Sha Tsui, exit B3)

Chang Won Korean Restaurant
KOREAN $$

19 Map p98, D1

One of the most authentic Korean restaurants in town, Chang Won makes delectable beef ribs, seafood pancakes and cold noodles, and the staff are generous with side dishes. But the toilet is not for the faint-hearted. (☎2368 4606; Kimberly St, 1G; lunch from HK$60, dinner from HK$100; � noon-4am; M Tsim Sha Tsui, exit B1)

Sweet Dynasty
CANTONESE, DESSERTS $

20 Map p98, C3

Sweet Dynasty's extensive menu encompasses a plethora of casual Cantonese dishes, but the desserts, noodles and congee, for which they became famous years ago, are still the best. The restaurant is clean and modern but gets crowded when busy. (糖朝; ☎2199 7799; 28 Hankow Rd, Shop A, Basement, Hong Kong Pacific Centre, Tsim Sha Tsui; meals HK$70-300; �is8am-midnight Mon-Thu, 8am-1am Fri, 7.30am-1am Sat, 7.30am-midnight Sun; ☖; M Tsim Sha Tsui, exit A1)

T'ang Court
CANTONESE, DIM SUM **$$$**

21 ✕ Map p98, B3

As befitting its name T'ang Court, with two Michelin stars, has mastered the art of fine Cantonese cooking. Deep-pile carpets, heavy silks and mindful staff contribute to a hushed atmosphere. If that seems too formal, rest assured, the polished service will make you feel right at home, like an emperor in his palace. The signature baked oysters with port require pre-ordering. (唐閣; ☏2375 1133; www.hongkong.langhamhotels.com; 8 Peking Rd, 1st, Langham Hotel, Tsim Sha Tsui; lunch HK$300-2000, dinner HK$500-2000; ☉noon-2.30pm & 6-10.30pm; 🚺; ☒Tsim Sha Tsui, exit L4)

Drinking

Butler
COCKTAIL BAR

22 🍷 Map p98, D3

A cocktail and whisky heaven hidden in the residential part of TST. You can flip through its whisky magazines as you watch bartender Uchida create magical concoctions with the flair and precision of a master mixologist in Ginza. We loved the cocktails made from fresh citruses. A discreet and welcome addition to the TST drinking scene. (☏2724 3828; 30 Mody Rd, 5th fl, Mody House, Tsim Sha Tsui; cover HK$200, snacks HK$30; ☉6.30pm-3am Mon-Fri, 6.30pm-2am Sat & Sun; ☒East Tsim Sha Tsui, exit N2)

Aqua Spirit
BAR

23 🍷 Map p98, B3

When night falls, you'll know why this über-fashionable bar has dim illumination and black furniture – the two-storey, floor-to-ceiling windows command sweeping views of the Hong Kong Island skyline that come to life after sundown. The tables by the windows are awesome for bringing a date. On the weekends, a DJ spins hip hop and lounge jazz. (☏3427 2288; www.aqua.com.hk; 1 Peking Rd, 29, 30th fl, Tsim Sha Tsui; ☉4pm-2am, happy hour 4-6pm; 🛜; ☒Tsm Sha Tsui, exit L5)

Tapas Bar
BAR

24 🍷 Map p98, E3

An intimate vibe and bistro-style decor make this a good place to unwind over champagne, tapas and the sports channel after a day of sightseeing. A table in the alfresco area will let you smoke and take in harbour views, visible beyond a river of cars. (☏2733 8756; www.shangri-la.com; 64 Mody Rd, Lobby, Kowloon Shangri-La, Tsim Sha Tsui; ☉3.30pm-1am Mon-Fri, from noon Sat & Sun; 🛜; ☒East Tsim Sha Tsui, exit P1)

InterContinental Lobby Lounge
BAR

25 🍷 Map p98, C4

Soaring plate glass and an unbeatable waterfront location make this one of the best spots to soak up that Hong Kong Island skyline and take in the busy harbour, although you pay for the privilege. It's also an ideal venue from

Understand

ABCs of Tao

During your stay in Hong Kong, you might see temples guarded by strongly coloured and fierce-looking gods. These are Taoist temples. Taoism is an indigenous Chinese religion originating in the shamanistic roots of Chinese civilisation. Though never declared a national religion, it thrived from the Tang to the Ming dynasties, and its influence has been ubiquitous in Chinese life. Unlike evangelical religions stressing crusading and personal conversion, Taoism addresses needs such as cures for illnesses, protection from evil spirits and funerary requirements. Unlike Buddhism, it does not attempt to sublimate the mundane.

Tao for the Road

In contemporary Hong Kong, construction projects, including those commissioned by the government and foreign-owned companies, are preceded by a ritual performed to appease the deities of nature, such as those ruling the earth. Offerings of fruit are piled on a makeshift shrine and incense sticks are lit. Similar rituals take place before the official shooting of a film or the opening of a new shop. It is believed that keeping the deities happy is important for health, safety and feng shui, the last a belief partly influenced by Taoism.

Tao for the Dead

The majority of funeral rites in Hong Kong are presided over by Taoist 'ritual specialists'. More colourful than Buddhist ceremonies, Taoist rites feature the continuous chanting of the scriptures to the rhythmic striking of *muyu* (a wooden, hand-held, slit drum) and elaborate procedures including the sprinkling of flowers on the ground to relieve bitterness.

Taoist Temples

During the first two weeks of the Lunar New Year, millions in Hong Kong pay their respects at Taoist temples. These tend to be more decorative than Buddhist places of worship, and there are no nuns or monks in the ones in Hong Kong, only the ritual specialists, who can marry and have children. Besides statues of mythical creatures in the temples, you'll see representations of the cypress (for friendship), the tortoise (for longevity), bamboo (for honour) and the bat (for divine blessing).

Top Tip

Learn Local Culture

One of the more interesting offerings from the Hong Kong Tourism Board (p194) is a series of a dozen free cultural programs in English called Cultural Kaleidoscope. Run by local experts in their fields, topics covered include antiques, architecture, Cantonese opera, Chinese medicine, Chinese cake making, Chinese tea, diamonds, feng shui, kung fu, jade and pearl shopping, and taichi.

which to watch the evening lightshow at 8pm. (☑2721 1211; www.hongkong-ic. intercontinental.com; 18 Salisbury Rd, Hotel InterContinental Hong Kong, Tsim Sha Tsui; ⏱24hr; ☎; Ⓜ East Tsim Sha Tsui, exit J)

Felix Bar
BAR

26 Map p98, C4

Enjoy the fabulous view at this Philippe Starck–designed bar in Hong Kong's poshest hotel. Guys, the view from the urinals in the gents' is just one reason to fill your bladders. (☑2315 3188; Salisbury Rd, 28th fl, Peninsula Hong Kong; ⏱6pm-2am; Ⓜ Tsim Sha Tsui, exit E)

Amuse
BAR

27 Map p98, D1

An airy bistro-like bar frequented by white-collar locals and university students who come for their draught beers, decent wines and funky cocktails. The best seats are the leather couches

next to a row of large windows; the communal table is great if you want to meet people; and the banquettes make for intimate tête-à-têtes. (☑2317 1988; 4 Austin Ave, Tsim Sha Tsui; ⏱5pm-4am Mon-Fri, 6pm-4am Sat, 6pm-3am Sun; ☎; Ⓜ Jordan, exit D)

Ozone
BAR

28 Map p98, A1

The highest bar in Asia has imaginative interiors, created to evoke a cyberesque Garden of Eden, with pillars resembling chocolate fountains in a hurricane and a myriad of refracted glass and colour-changing illumination. Equally dizzying is the wine list, with the most expensive bottle selling for over HK$150,000. Offers potential for a once-in-a-lifetime experience, in more ways than one. (☑2263 2263; www.ritzcarlton.com; 1 Austin Rd, 118th fl, ICC, Tsim Sha Tsui; ⏱5pm-1am Mon-Wed, to 2am Thu, to 3am Fri, 3pm-3am Sat, noon-midnight Sun; ☎; Ⓜ Kowloon, exit U3)

Ned Kelly's Last Stand
PUB

29 Map p98, B3

Named after a gun-toting Australian bushranger, Ned's is one of Hong Kong's oldest pubs. Most of the expat regulars here (and there are many) are drawn to the laid-back atmosphere and the Dixieland jazz band that plays and cracks jokes between songs. The bar is filled with old posters, rugby shirts and Oz-related paraphernalia. (☑2376 0562; 11A Ashley Rd, Tsim Sha Tsui; ⏱11.30am-2am, happy hour 11.30am-9pm; Ⓜ Tsim Sha Tsui, exit L5)

LONELY PLANET/GETTY IMAGES ©

Tea ceremony

Entertainment

Dada

LIVE MUSIC

30 ⭐ Map p98, C1

Located upstairs in a quirky hotel, Dada is an intimate cocktail bar decked out with florid wallpaper, plush velvet seats, and a couple of Dalí-esque paintings. Jazz and blues bands play here to a professional mid-30s crowd a few times a month. (39 Kimberley Rd, 2nd fl, Luxe Manor, Tsim Sha Tsui; ⊘11am-2am Mon-Sat, to 1am Sun; 🛜; MTsim Sha Tsui, exit B1)

Hong Kong Cultural Centre

THEATRE, MUSIC

31 ⭐ Map p98, B4

Hong Kong's premier arts perfor- mance venue, the world-class Cultural Centre contains a 2085-seat concert hall with an impressive Rieger pipe organ, two theatres and rehearsal studios. (香港文化中心; www.lcsd.gov.hk; 10 Salisbury Rd, Tsim Sha Tsui; ⊘9am-11pm; 🛜; MEast Tsim Sha Tsui, exit L6)

Shopping

BrownsTailor
MEN'S CLOTHING

32 🔒 Map p98, C2

Like Armoury (p40), BrownsTailor belongs to a new generation of bespoke tailoring shops for men. They're adept at both making traditional gentlemen's attire and instilling modern elements into a classic look. Depending on the fabric used, a suit can cost you anywhere between HK$4200 and HK$18,000. (📞 3996 8654; www.brownstailor.com; 88 Nathan Rd, Unit E, 2nd fl, Comfort Bldg, Tsim Sha Tsui; ⏱11am-7pm Mon-Fri, to 6.30pm Sat; Ⓜ Tsim Sha Tsui, exit B1)

Elements
MALL

33 🔒 Map p98, A1

Located inside the **ICC** (環球貿易廣場; www.shkp-icc.com), Kowloon's most upmarket shopping mall comprises five pleasant sections each decorated according to one of the five natural elements. Other thoughtful touches include good nursing facilities and helpful staff. Austin Rd West is an area built on reclaimed land that's connected to Austin Rd in Tsim Sha Tsui at its eastern end. (圓方; www.elementshk.com; 1 Austin Rd W, West Kowloon; ⏱11am-9pm; Ⓜ Kowloon, exit U3)

Initial
CLOTHING

This attractive shop and cafe (see 18 🍴 Map p98; D2) carries stylish, multifunctional urbanwear with European and Japanese influences.

The clothes created by local designers are complemented by imported shoes, bags and costume jewellery. (www.initialfashion.com; 48 Cameron Rd, Shop 2, Tsim Sha Tsui; ⏱11.30am-11.30pm; Ⓜ Tsim Sha Tsui, exit B2)

Curio Alley
GIFTS, SOUVENIRS

34 🔒 Map p98, C3

This is a fun place to rummage for name chops, soapstone carvings, fans and other Chinese bric-a-brac. It's found in an alleyway between Lock and Hankow Rds, just south of Haiphong Rd. (⏱10am-8pm; Ⓜ Tsim Sha Tsui, exit C1)

I.T.
CLOTHING, ACCESSORIES

35 🔒 Map p98, B3

I.T. carries a chic and edgy selection of first- to third-tier designer brands from Europe and Japan, with high but not outrageous price tags. The I.T. group has shops in almost all the major shopping areas in town. (www.ithk.com; 30 Canton Rd, Shop LG01 & LG16-17, Basement, Silvercord, Tsim Sha Tsui; ⏱11.30am-9pm; Ⓜ Tsim Sha Tsui, exit A1)

David Chan Photo Shop
PHOTOGRAPHY

36 🔒 Map p98, C2

If you've decided to give the digital age a miss altogether, or at least still use film cameras, this dealer is the most reputable used-camera shop in town. The owner David Chan has been working in the business since the 1960s and has some precious equipment in his collection. (陳烘相機; ☑ 2723 3886; 16 Kimberley Rd, Shop 15, ground fl, Champagne Court, Tsim Sha Tsui; ⏰ 10am-8pm Mon-Sat; Ⓜ Tsim Sha Tsui, exit B1)

Premier Jewellery

JEWELLERY

37 🔒 Map p98, C3

This third-generation family firm is directed by a qualified gemmologist. The range isn't huge but if you're looking for something particular, give Premier Jewellery a day's notice and a selection will be ready in time for your arrival. Staff can also help you design your own piece. (愛寶珠寶有限公司; ☑ 2368 0003; 50 Nathan Rd, Shop G14-15, ground fl, Holiday Inn Golden Mile Shopping Mall, Tsim Sha Tsui; ⏰ 10am-7.30pm Mon-Sat, to 4pm Sun; Ⓜ Tsim Sha Tsui, exit G)

Rise Shopping Arcade

CLOTHING

38 🔒 Map p98, D2

Bursting the seams of this minimall is cheap streetwear from Hong Kong, Korea and Japan, with a few knock-offs chucked in for good measure. Patience and a good eye could land you purchases fit for a *Vogue* photo shoot. It's best visited between 4pm and 8.30pm when most of the shops are open. (利時商場; www.rise-hk.com; 5-11 Granville Circuit, Tsim Sha Tsui; ⏰ 3-9pm; Ⓜ Tsim Sha Tsui, exit B2)

Swindon Books

BOOKS

39 🔒 Map p98, C3

This is one of the best 'real' (as opposed to 'supermarket') bookshops.

Top Tip

Beware: Fake Monks

Real monks never solicit money. During your stay, however, you may be approached in temples, even in bars and shops at any time of the day, by con artists in monks' habits who will try to make you part with your money. The more aggressive ones may offer fake Buddhist amulets for sale, or force 'blessings' on you then pester you for a donation. Many speak Putonghua (standard Chinese) and a few words of English. When accosted, just tell them 'no' and ignore them.

An excellent range and knowledgeable staff. Strong on local books and history in particular. (☑ 2366 8001; 13-15 Lock Rd, Tsim Sha Tsui; ⏰ 9am-6pm Mon-Fri, to 1pm Sat; Ⓜ Tsim Sha Tsui, exit A1)

Ocean Terminal

SHOPPING CENTRE

40 🔒 Map p98, A4

Located to the north of the clock tower on Salisbury Rd is Star House, a frayed-looking retail and office complex. At its western end is the entrance to Ocean Terminal, the long building jutting into the harbour. It is part of the massive Harbour City shopping complex that stretches for half a kilometre north along Canton Rd and offers priceless views of Tsim Sha Tsui's western waterfront. (☑ 24 hr hotline 2118 8666; www.harbourcity.com.hk; Salisbury Rd; ⏰ 10am-9pm; 🚢 Star Ferry)

Explore

Kowloon: Yau Ma Tei & Mong Kok

Yau Ma Tei – meaning the place *(tei)* where fishermen waterproofed boats with oil *(yau)* and repaired hemp ropes *(ma)* – rewards the explorer with a close-up look at a more traditional Hong Kong. Congested Mong Kok (Prosperous Point) teems with shops selling electronics, clothes, shoes, jewellery and kitchen supplies, but a few cultural oases have also emerged in the area.

Sights in a Day

Have breakfast at **Mido Café** (p120) in Yau Ma Tei. Replenished, explore **Tin Hau Temple** (p117), the **Jade Market** (p117), and **Yau Ma Tei Theatre** (p117), then stroll down **Shanghai Street** (p117), poking your head into the traditional shops. All this should take around two hours. Have lunch at **Nathan Congee and Noodle** (p119).

Go see the beautiful **Lui Seng Chun** (p118) building and **C&G Artpartment** (p118) in Mong Kok. If there's time, check out the speciality malls in **Mong Kok**.

Have dinner at **Temple Street Night Market** (p114). Then it's on to **Canton Singing House** (p122) for some old-fashioned revelry.

◉ Top Sights

Temple Street Night Market (p114)

♥ Best of Hong Kong

Shopping

Bruce Lee Club (p122)

Sino Centre (p123)

Hong Kong Reader (p122)

Mong Kok Computer Centre (p123)

Markets

Temple Street Night Market (p114)

Wholesale Fruit Market (p118)

Jade Market (p117)

Tung Choi Street Market (p123)

Getting There

Ⓜ **Metro** Jordan, Yau Ma Tei and Mong Kok stations (Tsuen Wan line).

🚌 **Bus** 2, 6, 6A and 9.

Top Sights
Temple Street Night Market

The liveliest night market in Hong Kong, Temple St extends from Man Ming Lane to Nanking St and is cut in two by Tin Hau Temple. It's a great place to go for the bustling atmosphere, the aromas and tastes on offer from the food stalls, the occasional free Cantonese opera performance, and some shopping and fortune telling.

◉ Map p116, B4

廟街夜市

Yau Ma Tei

🕓 6-11pm

Ⓜ Yau Ma Tei, exit C

Dining at Temple Street Night Market

Don't Miss

Shopping

While you may find better bargains over the border in Shēnzhèn, it's more fun to shop here. The stalls are crammed with cheap clothes, watches, pirated CDs, fake labels, footwear, cookware, and everyday items. Any marked prices should be considered suggestions – this is definitely a place to bargain.

Street Food

For al fresco dining head to Woo Sung St, which runs parallel to the east, or to the section of Temple St north of the temple. You can get anything from a bowl of noodles to Chiu Chow–style oyster omelettes and Nepalese curries, costing anywhere from HK$30 to HK$300. There are also quite a few seafood and hotpot restaurants in the area.

Fortune Telling

Every evening a gaggle of fortune tellers sets up tents in the middle of the market; by reading your face, palm or date of birth, they'll make predictions about your life (consultations from HK$100). Some keep birds that have been trained to pick out 'fortune' cards. Questions of accuracy aside, it's all quite entertaining. Most of them speak some English.

Cantonese Opera

If you're in luck, you'll catch an extract of a Cantonese opera performed under the stars. Some of the most famous divas and maestros of the opera stage began their careers in this humble fashion (or so they say).

☑ **Top Tips**

▶ The market is at its best from 7pm to 10pm, when it's clogged with stalls and people.

✕ **Take a Break**

Mido Café (p120) has cheap local grub and a cool retro vibe. If it's full, head to nearby Kubrick Bookshop Café (p122) for light bites and coffee.

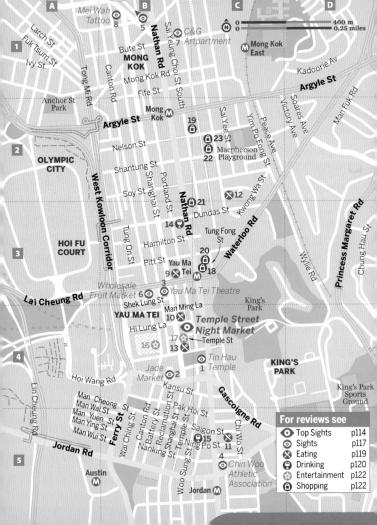

A   B   C   D

Larch St
Fuk Tsum St
Ivy St

Mei Wah
Tattoo 8

5

C&G 7
Artpartment

Mong Kok
East

Kadoorie Av

Bute St
Canton Rd
Tong Mi Rd
Nathan Rd

**MONG
KOK**

Mong Kok Rd

Sai Yeung Choi St South

Argyle St

Fife St

Anchor St
Park

Argyle St

Mong Kok 19

Sai Yee St

**OLYMPIC
CITY**

Nelson St

23
22 Macpherson
Playground

Victory Ave

Soares Ave

Peace Ave

Yim Po Fong St

Man Fuk Rd

West Kowloon Corridor

Shantung St

Soy St

Shanghai St

Portland St

Nathan Rd

21
14

12

Dundas St

Kwong Wa St

**HOI FU
COURT**

Tung On St

Hamilton St

Tung Fong
St

Waterloo Rd

Princess Margaret Rd

Chung Hau St

20

Pitt St

Yau Ma
9 Tei 18

Wylie Rd

Lai Cheung Rd

Wholesale
Fruit Market 6

3
Yau Ma Tei Theatre

Shek Lung St

King's
Park

YAU MA TEI

Man Ming La

10

Temple Street
Night Market

Hi Lung La

16

17
13

Temple St

**KING'S
PARK**

Tin Hau
1 Temple

Jade
Market 2

Hoi Wang Rd

Man Cheong St
Man Wai St
Man Yuen St
Man Ying St
Man Wui St

Ferry St

Wai Ching St

Canton Rd

Battery St

Reclamation St

Shanghai St

Temple St

Pak Hoi St

Kansu St

Gascoigne Rd

Saigon St

15

Ning Po St

11

Chi Wo St

King's Park
Sports
Ground

Lin Cheung Rd

Jordan Rd

Nanking St

Woo Sung St

4
Chin Woo
Athletic
Association

Austin

Jordan

0   400 m
0   0.25 miles

For reviews see	
◎ Top Sights	p114
◎ Sights	p117
✕ Eating	p119
🍸 Drinking	p120
★ Entertainment	p122
🛍 Shopping	p122

Sights

Tin Hau Temple

TEMPLE

1 Map p116, C4

This large, incense-filled sanctuary built in the 19th century is one of Hong Kong's most famous Tin Hau (Goddess of the Sea) temples. The public square out front is Yau Ma Tei's communal heart where fishermen once laid out their hemp ropes to sun next to Chinese banyans that today shade chess players and elderly men. Yau Ma Tei Police Station is a listed blue-and-white structure one block to the east along Public Square St. (天后廟; ☎2385 0759; www.ctc. org.hk; cnr Temple St & Public Square St, Yau Ma Tei; ⏱8am-5pm; Ⓜ Yau Ma Tei, exit C)

Jade Market

MARKET

2 Map p116, B4

The covered Jade Market, split into two parts by Battery St, has hundreds of stalls selling all varieties and grades of jade. But unless you really know your nephrite from your jadeite, it's not wise to buy expensive pieces here. (玉器市場; Battery St & Kansu St, Yau Ma Tei; ⏱10am-6pm; Ⓜ Yau Ma Tei, exit C)

Yau Ma Tei Theatre

BUILDING

3 Map p116, B3

Yau Ma Tei Theatre (1920) with art-deco interiors, and adjacent to the Wholesale Fruit Market, had for decades kept coolies and rickshaw drivers entertained, but losing business to modern cinemas in the '80s, it began showing

Local Life

Shanghai Street

Starting from Kansu St, a stroll down **Shanghai Street** (Map p116, B2; 上海街; Yau Ma Tei; Ⓜ Yau Ma Tei, exit C) will take you back to a time long past. Once Kowloon's main drag, it's flanked by stores selling embroidered Chinese bridal gowns, sandalwood incense, kitchenware, Buddha statues, a pawn shop (at the corner of Saigon St), and mah-jong parlours. It's a great place to shop for unusual souvenirs or a Buddhist home shrine if you ever need one. For a break, nip across Nathan Rd via an underground walkway for low-price, high-quality staples at Nathan Congee and Noodle (p119).

erotic films and selling porn videos to stay afloat. At 8 Waterloo Rd next door, the neoclassical **Red Brick House** (紅磚屋) once belonged to a pumping station (1895). The buildings now house a Cantonese opera performance and training centre. (油麻地戲院; ☎2264 8108, tickets 2374 2598; www.lcsd.gov.hk/ymtt; 6 Waterloo Rd, cnr Waterloo Rd & Reclamation St, Yau Ma Tei; Ⓜ Yau Ma Tei, exit B2)

Chin Woo Athletic Association

MARTIAL ARTS SCHOOL

4 Map p116, C5

This is the 88-year-old branch of the Chin Woo Athletic Association, founded 100 years ago in Shanghai by the famed kung-fu master Huo Yuanjia (霍元甲). The Shanghai school was

Local Life

Sing-Along Parlours

A highlight of Yau Ma Tei is its old-fashioned sing-along parlours (歌廳) like Canton Singing House (p122). They started 20 years ago as shelter for street singers on rainy days.

Most parlours have basic setups – tables, a stage, and Christmas lights for an upbeat atmosphere. All have their own organist and troupe of freelance singers – ladies who'll keep you company and persuade you to make a dedication or sing along with them for a fee. Their repertoire spans from Chinese operatic extracts to English oldies. You'll see many regulars at these places.

It's more fun to go after 9pm. As parlours don't provide food, you're welcome to order delivery. Some sell beer, but you can also get your own from convenience stores.

featured in Bruce Lee's *Fist of Fury* and Jet Li's *Fearless*. You can visit the school during opening hours. Classes, however, are taught mainly in Cantonese. (精武體育館; ☏2384 3238; 300 Nathan Rd, flat B & C, 13th fl, Wah Fung Bldg, Yau Ma Tei; ◷2.30-9pm; Ⓜ Jordan, exit B1)

Lui Seng Chun   HISTORIC BUILDING

5 ◎ Map p116, B1

Hugging a street corner is this beautiful four-storey Chinese 'shophouse' (c 1931) belonging to a school of Chinese medicine. It features a mix of Chinese and European architectural styles – deep verandahs, urn-shaped balustrades and

other fanciful takes on a neoclassical Italian villa. The ground floor, which has a herbal tea shop, is open to public. Free guided tours to the upper-floor clinics is available by registration. They're in Cantonese, but exhibits have bilingual labels. (雷春生堂; ☏3411 0628; http://scm.hkbu.edu.hk/lsctour; 119 Lai Chi Kok Rd, cnr Lai Chi Kok & Tong Mi Rds; admission free; ◷guided tour 2.30pm & 4pm Mon-Fri, 9.30am & 11am Sat; consultation 9am-1pm & 2-8pm Mon-Sat, 9am-1pm Sun; Ⓜ Prince Edward, exit C2)

Wholesale Fruit Market   MARKET

6 ◎ Map p116, B3

This historic and still operating market, founded in 1913, is a cluster of one- or two-storey brick and stone buildings with pre-WWII signboards. It is a hive of activity from 4am to 6am when fresh fruit is loaded on and off trucks, and bare-backed workers manoeuvre piles of boxes under the moon. The market is bounded by Ferry St, Waterloo Rd and Reclamation St with Shek Lung St running through it. To get here from Yau Ma Tei MTR exit B2, turn right. (油麻地果欄; cnr Shek Lung St & Reclamation St, Yau Ma Tei; ◷2-6am; Ⓜ Yau Ma Tei, exit B2)

C&G Artpartment   GALLERY

7 ◎ Map p116, B1

Clara and Gum, the founders of this edgy art space behind the Pioneer Centre (始創中心) are passionate about nurturing the local art scene and representing socially minded artists. They close late when there are events. See website for the latest. (📞2390 9332; www.candg-artpartment.com; 222 Sai Yeung Choi St S, 3rd fl, Mong Kok; 🕐2-7.30pm Thu, Fri, Sun & Mon, from 11am Sat; Ⓜ Prince Edward, exit B2)

Mei Wah Tattoo   TATTOO PARLOUR

 8 Map p116, B1

Tattoo artist and avid traveller Nic Tse is Chinese but speaks perfect English. We were impressed by his repertoire, which includes abstract contemporary designs, lines of poetry, interpretations of childhood dreams and minimalist armscapes. Interested parties should email Nic as early as possible to discuss specifics and book. Payment is in cash or via PayPal. (美華刺青; 📞2757 0027, 6333 5352; kowloonink@gmail.com; 703 Shanghai St, 4th fl, Mong Kok; per hr HK$1000; Ⓜ Prince Edward, exit C1)

Eating

Sun Sin   NOODLES $

 9 Map p116, B3

A Michelin-praised brisket shop in a 'hood known for brothels, Sun Sin has kept quality up and prices down despite its laurel. The succulent cuts of meat are served in a broth with radish, in a chunky tomato soup, or as a curry. At peak times, makeshift tables are available upstairs for those who prize food over comfort. (新仙清湯腩; 📞2332 6872; 37 Portland St, Yau Ma Tei; meals HK$40-65; 🕐11am-midnight; Ⓜ Yau Ma Tei, exit B2)

Good Hope Noodle (p120)

Hing Kee Restaurant   DAI PAI DONG, CANTONESE $

10 Map p116, B4

Previously a roadside stall that started out by whipping up hearty claypot rice and oyster omelettes (HK$20) for night revellers and Triads, Hing Kee now serves the same under a roof but without the atmosphere. (興記菜館; 📞2384 3647; 19 Temple St; 🕐6pm-1am; Ⓜ Yau Ma Tei, exit C)

Nathan Congee and Noodle   CONGEE, NOODLES $

11 Map p116, C5

This low-key eatery has been making great congee and noodles for the last

Top Tip
Upstairs Mong Kok

Mong Kok can be intense. After all, it is the most densely populated spot on the face of the earth. To experience energetic MK without the insanity, make a beeline for its upstairs spaces. Above-ground oases include C&G Artpartment (p118), Hong Kong Reader (p122), Fullcup Café and Bruce Lee Club (p122).

stands astride a street corner that comes to life at sundown. Ascend to the upper floor and take a seat next to a wall of iron-framed windows overlooking Tin Hau Temple (p117) – atmosphere is what makes it Kowloon's most famous tea cafe, despite passable food and service. (美都餐室; ☑2384 6402; 63 Temple St; meals HK$40-90; ◷9am-10pm; Ⓜ Yau Ma Tei, exit B2)

Drinking

Fullcup Café
CAFE

 14 Map p116, B3

'Full cup' sounds similar to the Cantonese for 'breathe' and it's what this quirky three-storey cafe does – offer a breather in the midst of Mong Kok. With retro furniture and an alfresco space, it attracts a young local artsy crowd. Fullcup serves decent coffee, smoothies and beer. There are live gigs on some weekends. (呼吸咖啡茶館; 36 Dundas St, 4-6th fl, Hanwai Commercial Centre, Mong Kok; ◷noon-3am; 🛜; Ⓜ Yau Ma Tei, exit A1)

half-century. Order a side of fritters (to be dunked into congee and eaten slightly soggy), try a rice dumpling, or taste the blanched fish skin tossed with parsley and peanuts. (彌敦粥麵家; ☑2771 4285; 11 Saigon St, Yau Ma Tei; meals HK$60; ◷7.30am-11.30pm; Ⓜ Jordan, exit B2)

Good Hope Noodle
NOODLES $

12 Map p116, C2

Despite a relocation and makeover, this 40-year-old shop has managed to retain its Michelin commendation and fan following. Now al dente egg noodles, bite-sized wontons, and silky congee that have won hearts for decades continue to be cooked the old way, but are served in neat, modern surrounds. (好旺角麵家; ☑2384 6898; 18 Fa Yuen St, Shop 5-6, Mong Kok; meals HK$30-90; ◷11am-12.45am; Ⓜ Mong Kok, exit D3)

Mido Café
CAFE $

13 Map p116, B4

This retro *cha chaan tang* (1950) with mosaic tiles and metal latticework

Snake King Yan
SNAKE BILE

 15 Map p116, C5

Challenge yourself to a shot of rice wine mixed with snake bile at this speciality shop near the Temple Street Night Market (p114). If that reviles you, there are jars of exotic infusions on display that you might prefer. Snake bile is believed to increase virility. (蛇王恩; ☑2384 5608; 80A Woo Sung St, Yau Ma Tei; ◷noon-10pm; Ⓜ Jordan, exit A)

Understand
Hong Kong Occult

Feng Shui

Literally meaning 'wind water', feng shui (or geomancy) aims to balance the elements of nature to create a harmonious environment. It's been practiced since the 12th century, and it continues to influence the design of everything from high-rises to highways in Hong Kong. To guard against evil forces, which gain momentum when travelling in a straight line, doors are often positioned at an angle to each other. Ideally, homes and businesses should have a view of calm water – even a fish tank helps. Corporate executives shouldn't have offices that face west, otherwise their profits will go in the same direction as the setting sun.

Fortune Telling

A common method of divination in Hong Kong is the use of *chim* – the bamboo 'fortune sticks' found at temples. You shake a canister filled with these sticks until one falls to the ground. All the while, you contemplate a problem that's been bothering you. Each stick bears a numeral corresponding to lines of poetry printed on a slip of paper held by the temple guardian. You take the fallen stick to the temple guardian to redeem the piece of paper. You then ask the temple's fortune teller to interpret the poetic lines for you. Supposedly they're the answer to your problem.

Zodiac

The Chinese zodiac has 12 signs as does the Western one, but their representations are all animals. Your sign is based on the year of your birth (according to the Chinese lunar calendar). Being born or married in a particular year is believed to contribute to one's fortune. The year of the dragon sees the biggest jump in the birth rate, closely followed by the year of the tiger. Babies born in these years are believed to become noble and fearless leaders.

Local Life
Cutlery Store

At **Chan Wah Kee Cutlery Store**
(Map p116, B5; 陳華記刀莊; ☑2730
4091; Temple St, 278D, Yau Ma Tei;
⊙11am-6pm, closed Wed; M Jordan, exit
C2) you can watch one of Asia's last
remaining master knife-sharpeners
in action. Eighty-year-old Mr Chan
uses nine different stones to grind
each blade, alternating between
water and oil. His clients include
chefs, butchers, tailors and domestic gourmands from all over the
world. Customers have sent him
their Japanese willow knives for
his magic touch. Mr Chan charges
between HK$100 and HK$600 to
sharpen a blade, with a wait time
of three months. However, if you buy
a knife from his good selection, he'll
sharpen it there and then. Prices
range from HK$200 for a paring
knife to HK$2000 for a Shun knife.

Entertainment

Broadway Cinematheque CINEMA

16 ⭐ Map p116, B4

The place for new art-house releases
and rerun screenings. The **Kubrick
Bookshop Café** (☑2384 8929; www.
kubrick.com.hk; 3 Public Square St, Shop H2,
Prosperous Garden, Yau Ma Tei; ⊙11.30am-
9.30pm; M Yau Ma Tei, exit C) next door
serves decent coffee and simple meals.
(百老匯電影中心; ☑2388 3188; 3 Public
Square St, ground fl, Prosperous Gardens, Yau
Ma Tei; M Yau Ma Tei, exit C)

Canton Singing House LIVE MUSIC

17 ⭐ Map p116, B4

The oldest and most atmospheric of
the sing-along parlours (p118), Canton
resembles a film set with its mirror
balls and glowing shrines. Each session features 20 singers, all with fan
following. Patrons tip a minimum
of HK$20 (per patron) if they like a
song. But even if you don't, it's nice to
tip every now and then for the experience – just slip your money into a box
on stage. For HK$100, you can sing
a song. (艷陽天; 49-51 Temple St, Yau Ma
Tei; entrance HK$20; ⊙3-7pm & 8pm-5am;
M Yau Ma Tei, exit C)

Shopping

Bruce Lee Club SOUVENIRS

18 🔒 Map p116, C3

Founded by Bruce Lee's fans, this
mini-museum and souvenir shop has
action figures, toys, movie products
and other memorabilia related to the
kung-fu icon. (李小龍會; ☑2771 7093;
www.bruceleeclub.com; 530 Nathan Rd, Shop
160-161, In's Point, Mong Kok; admission free;
⊙1-9pm; M Yau Ma Tei, exit A1)

Hong Kong Reader BOOKS

19 🔒 Map p116, C2

Run by a handful of young people,
this is a bilingual bookstore-cafe with
an intellectual bent. If you're looking
for the likes of Derrida or Milosz, this
is the place to go. Check the website

for the latest literary readings, though most are conducted in Cantonese. Hong Kong Reader is above a 1010 telecommunications shop. (序言書室; ☎2395 0031; www.hkreaders.com; 68 Sai Yeung Choi St S, 7th fl, Mong Kok; ☺2pm-midnight; Ⓜ Mong Kok, exit D3)

Protrek
OUTDOOR EQUIPMENT

20 🔒 Map p116, C3

This reliable shop with branches all over town is arguably your best bet for outdoor gear that will see you through from sea to summit. It runs training courses on outdoor activities as well. The English-speaking staff are very helpful. (保捷行; www.protrek.com.hk; 5 Tung Fong St, Yau Ma Tei; ☺noon-8pm Mon-Sat, 11.30am-9.30pm Sun; Ⓜ Yau Ma Tei, exit C)

Sino Centre
MALL

21 🔒 Map p116, B3

This shabby go-to place for all things related to Asian animation and comics will give you a taste of local culture. Its tiny shops carry new and back issues of Japanese manga, action figures, old-fashioned video games and other kidult bait that attract a largely male following. (信和中心; 582-592 Nathan Rd, Mong Kok; ☺10am-10pm; Ⓜ Yau Ma Tei, exit A2)

Tung Choi St Market
MARKET

22 🔒 Map p116, C2

The Tung Choi St market is a cheek-by-jowl affair offering cheap clothes and trinkets. Vendors start setting up their stalls as early as noon, but it's best to get here between 1pm and 6pm when there's much more on offer. Beware, the sizes stocked here tend to suit the lissom Asian frame. (通菜街, 女人街, Ladies' Market; Tung Choi St; ☺noon-11.30pm; Ⓜ Mong Kok, exit D3)

Mong Kok Computer Centre
MALL

23 🔒 Map p116, C2

Prices at this computer mall are cheap but language can be a barrier, and you'll see more finished products than computer components. (旺角電腦中心; 8-8A Nelson St, Mong Kok; ☺1-10pm; Ⓜ Mong Kok, exit D3)

Top Sights
Sik Sik Yuen Wong Tai Sin Temple

Getting There

The temple is north of Wong Tai Sin MTR station, in the middle of the Wong Tai Sin area.

Ⓜ **MTR** Wong Tai Sin, exit B2

A sensory whirl of roofs and pillars, intricate latticework, bridges, flowers and incense, this bustling Taoist temple, built in 1973, has something for all walks of Hong Kong society, from pensioners and tycoons to parents and young professionals. Some come simply to pray and thank the deity, some to divine their future, others to get hitched – Sik Sik Yuen is an appointed temple for Taoist weddings.

Sik Sik Yuen Wong Tai Sin Temple

Don't Miss

The Deity

Wong Tai Sin was a shepherd who was said to have transformed boulders into sheep. When he was 15, an immortal taught him how to make a potion that could cure all illnesses; he is thus worshipped by the sick and the health-conscious. The term 'Wong Tai Sin' is sometimes used to describe those who are generous to a fault.

Main Altar

The main altar is where ceremonies take place. The image of the deity was brought here from Guǎngdōng province in 1915. Behind the main altar are the **Good Wish Gardens** (admission by donation HK$2; ⏰9am-4pm), replete with pavilions and carp ponds.

Fortune Telling

To the left of the entrance is an arcade of fortune tellers (consultations from HK$100), some of whom speak English. You can also divine your future with *chim* – bamboo 'fortune sticks' that are shaken out of a box on to the ground and then interpreted by a fortune teller.

Nearby: Chi Lin Nunnery

Just one MTR stop away from the temple is this arresting Buddhist **nunnery** (志蓮淨苑; ☎2354 1888; www.chilin.org; 5 Chi Lin Dr, Diamond Hill; admission free; ⏰nunnery 9am-4.30pm, garden 6.30am-7pm; Ⓜ Diamond Hill, exit C2), rebuilt completely of wood in 1998 – with not a single nail – in the style of a Tang dynasty monastery.

Also in the complex is **Chi Lin Vegetarian** (志蓮素齋, 龍門樓, Long Men Lou; ☎3658 9388; 60 Fung Tak Rd, Nan Lian Garden; meals from HK$200; ⏰noon-9pm Mon-Fri, 11.30am-9pm Sat & Sun; ☝; Ⓜ Diamond Hill, exit C2), an excellent restaurant.

嗇色園黃大仙祠

www.siksikyuen.org.hk

2, Chuk Yuen Village, Wong Tai Sin

donation HK$2

⏰7am-5.30pm

☑ Top Tips

▶ Colourful ceremonies take place in the main altar; call for times.

▶ Nearby gadget heaven, **Ap Liu Street Flea Market** (鴨寮街; Ap Liu St, btwn Nam Cheong & Yen Chow Sts, Sham Shui Po; ⏰noon-midnight; Ⓜ Sham Shui Po, exit A1); artists' studios at **Jockey Club Creative Arts Centre** (賽馬會創意藝術中心, JCCAC; www.jccac.org.hk; 30 Pak Tin St, Shek Kip Mei; ⏰10am-10pm; Ⓜ Shek Kip Mei, exit C).

✖ Take a Break

Fullcup Café (☎3728 3454; 70 Berwick St, Block 41, Shek Kip Mei Estate, Sham Shui Po; HK$30-60; ⏰7am-11pm; ☎; ▣A21, Ⓜ Sham Shui Po, exit D2) serves good local fast food in a faux-retro setting.

Explore

New Territories

Along with Lantau, the New Territories contain the rural and wild places of Hong Kong. Given the close proximity of seven million people, that might sound like an odd claim, but you really can get away from the city here. Extensive country parks, a world-class museum, interesting temples and a wetland park are among the worthwhile attractions in this area.

The Sights in a Day

☀ Get up early and make your way to **Ping Shan Heritage Trail** (p133) in Yuen Long to see a magnificent walled village. Have lunch at **Tai Wing Wah** (p134) in the town of Yuen Long and check out the neighbourhood.

☀ Make your way to **Sai Kung** (p133) in New Territories East. Explore the shops in the town and the fishing boats by the pier. Have afternoon tea at **Honeymoon Dessert** (p134) if you're hungry.

☾ If there's time, take the bus to Sha Tin to spend an hour at the **Hong Kong Heritage Museum** (p132). Have dinner at **Sha Tin 18** (p134), just outside University MTR Station, or make your way to Kowloon or Hong Kong Island for dinner and drinks.

For a local's day of hiking in the New Territories, see p128.

 Local Life

Hiking in the New Territories (p128)

 Best of Hong Kong

Temples
Tsing Shan Monastery (p132)

Activities
Tai Long Wan Trail (p129)

High Island Reservoir East Dam Trail (p128)

Bride's Pool – Lai Chi Wo (p129)

Getting There

Ⓜ **Metro** East and West Rail lines; Light Rail Transit (LRT) lines.

🚌 **Bus Kowloon Motor Bus Co** (KMB; ☎ 2745 4466; www.kmb.hk) and green minibuses fill gaps left by the MTR network.

Local Life
Hiking in the New Territories

Some of Hong Kong's best hiking trails pass lofty peaks, wave-lapped coves, rustic hamlets, sprawling reserves and handsome reservoirs in the New Territories. Here are some picturesque routes favoured by locals; each is a suggestion for half a day's hike. For more, see www.hkwalkers. net. The Map Publications Centre (www.landsd.gov.hk/mapping/en/ pro&ser/products.htm) has maps detailing trails.

❶ **High Island Reservoir East Dam Trail (**萬宜水庫東壩遠足徑**; 3–5 hours)**
Surreal and dramatic, High Island Reservoir East Dam (萬宜水庫東壩) has massive dolosse (anchor-shaped blocks), slanting volcanic columns and sapphire waters. Five-hour route: take bus 94 from Sai Kung town to Pak Tam Chung (北潭涌), walk to East Dam (9km, two hours via Tai Mong Tsai and Man Yee Rds), hike the trail (1km, 30

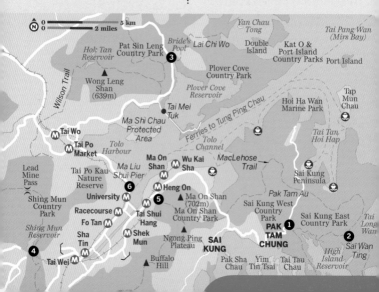

minutes) then walk back. Three-hour route (advised): taxi from Sai Kung to East Dam (HK$130, 25 minutes), hike the trail and walk to Pak Tam Chung.

❷ Tai Long Wan Trail
(大浪灣遠足徑; 4 hours)
This moderately challenging 12km trail passes delicious, swim-worthy bays (Sai Wan, Ham Tin, Chek Keng). Take bus 29R at Chan Man Rd (Sai Kung town), disembarking at the last stop, Sai Wan Ting (西灣亭); or take a taxi (HK$110). From the exit in Pak Tam Au (北潭凹), minibuses go back to Sai Kung.

❸ Bride's Pool – Lai Chi Wo
(荔枝窩 – 新娘潭; 4½ hours)
This challenging 12km heritage and biodiversity trail passes mangrove forests and a huge Hakka village backed by an ancient 'feng shui' wood. Bride's Pool is a pool (潭) hemmed in by rocks below a waterfall. Route: Bride's Pool – Wu Kau Tang – Sam A Tsuen – Lai Chi Wo – Fan Shui Au – Bride's Pool Rd. At the bus terminus at Tai Po Market MTR station, catch bus 75K to Tai Mei Tuk (大美督) terminus, and from there, cab it to Bride's Pool (HK$80).

❹ Shing Mun Reservoir Trail
(城門水塘遠足徑; 3 hours)
This easy 9.5km trail loops around Shing Mun Reservoir, passing a dappled country park and a valley with a gushing stream and travelling through silent, almost magical, paper-bark forests. Take minibus 82 to Shiu Wo St (Tsuen Wan) and walk 20 minutes to Pineapple Dam (菠蘿壩). Go back the same way.

❺ Ma On Shan Country Park Trail
(馬鞍山郊遊徑; 2½ hours)
This 4.5km trail runs past an old iron miners' settlement, up to the idyllic butterfly haven Ngong Ping Plateau (昂平), then to the villages of Tai Shui Tseng (大水井). Take the MTR to Heng On station, walk for about six minutes to the Heng On Estate roundabout, then another 45 minutes to the entrance of the park. The exit is a short walk on Po Lo Che Rd to Sai Kung.

❻ Tung Ping Chau Walking Trail
(東平洲步行徑; 2 hours)
This easy 6km hike around Hong Kong's deserted eastern island features eccentric rock layers, wave-beaten grottoes, lovely sea shards and waters teeming with corals and sea anemones. **Tsui Wah Ferry Services** (☎ 2527 2513, 2272 2022; www.traway.com. hk) runs ferries here (Saturday, Sunday and public holidays) from Ma Liu Shui pier, near University station.

A **B** **C** **D**

1

SHENZHEN

Lo Wu

Lok Ma
Chau

For reviews see
Sights   p132
Eating   p133

0   5 km
0   2.5 miles

Mai Po
4 Nature
Reserve

2

Hong Kong
3 Wetland Park

Lam Tseun North
Country Park

Long
Ping

8

**NEW
TERRITORIES**

Tin Shui
Wai   5   Yuen
Ping Shan   Long
Heritage
Trail

Kam Sheung Rd

3

Siu
Hong

Tuen
Mun   1

Tsing Shan
Monastery

Tai Lam
Country
Park

Tai Mo Shan
Country
Park

MacLehose Trail

Tai Lam
Tunnel

4

7

Tai Lam Chung
Reservoir

9

Tsuen Wan
West

5

East
Brother

Ma
Wan

Tsing Ma
Bridge

Kap Shui Mun
Bridge

Lantau

Tsing Yi

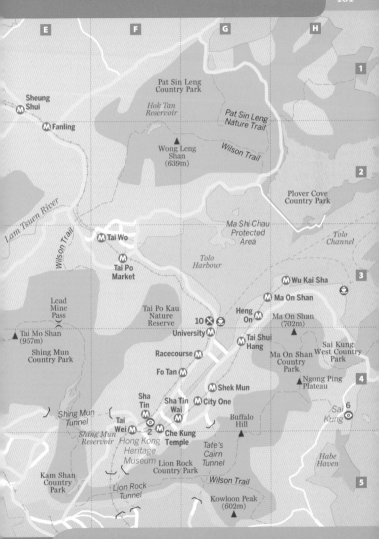

E | F | G | H

1

Sheung Shui Ⓜ
Ⓜ Fanling

Pat Sin Leng Country Park
Hok Tan Reservoir
Pat Sin Leng Nature Trail
Wilson Trail
▲ Wong Leng Shan (639m)

2

Plover Cove Country Park

Lam Tsuen River

Wilson Trail

Ⓜ Tai Wo
Ⓜ Tai Po Market

Ma Shi Chau Protected Area

Tolo Harbour

Tolo Channel

3

Lead Mine Pass

▲ Tai Mo Shan (957m)

Shing Mun Country Park

Tai Po Kau Nature Reserve

10 ⊗
University Ⓜ

Racecourse Ⓜ

Fo Tan Ⓜ

Ⓜ Wu Kai Sha

Ⓜ Ma On Shan

Heng On Ⓜ

Ⓜ Tai Shui Hang

Ma On Shan (702m) ▲

Ma On Shan Country Park

Sai Kung West Country Park

4

▲ Ngong Ping Plateau

Sai Kung 6 ◎

Shing Mun Tunnel

Shing Mun Reservoir

Tai Wei Ⓜ
2

Sha Tin Ⓜ
Sha Tin Wai Ⓜ

Ⓜ City One

Ⓜ Shek Mun

Che Kung Temple

Hong Kong Heritage Museum

Buffalo Hill ▲

Kam Shan Country Park

Lion Rock Tunnel

Lion Rock Country Park

Tate's Cairn Tunnel

Wilson Trail

▲ Kowloon Peak (602m)

Habe Haven

5

Sights

Tsing Shan Monastery
BUDDHIST MONASTERY

1 Map p130, A4

This temple complex perched on the hill of Castle Peak is the oldest in Hong Kong. Founded by Reverend Pui To 1500 years ago, the complex you see today was rebuilt in 1926. Check out shrines and temples for different saints and bodhisattvas, including one to Pui To in a grotto, as you ascend the hill. Some of these have slid into dilapidation; nonetheless they're imbued with a spooky charm. (Castle Peak Monastery, 青山禪院; ☑2461 8050; Tsing Shan Monastery Path; ☺24hr; ☒line 610, 615, 615P)

Hong Kong Heritage Museum
MUSEUM

2 Map p130, F4

Southwest of Sha Tin town centre, this spacious, high-quality museum gives a peek into local history and culture. Highlights include a children's area with interactive play zones, the New Territories Heritage Hall with mock-ups of traditional minority villages, the Cantonese Opera Heritage Hall, where you can watch old operas with English subtitles, and an elegant gallery of Chinese art. Lately, the big draw is a semi-permanent Bruce Lee exhibit, with some 600 items of memorabilia on display until 2018. (香港文化博物館; ☑2180 8188; www.heritagemuseum.gov.hk; 1 Man Lam Rd; adult/concession HK$10/5, Wed

free; ☺10am-6pm Mon & Wed-Sat, to 7pm Sun; ☒; Ⓜ Che Kung Temple)

Hong Kong Wetland Park
PARK

3 Map p130, B2

This 60-hectare ecological park is a window on the wetland ecosystems of northwest New Territories. The natural trails, bird hides and viewing platforms make it a handy and excellent spot for bird-watching. The futuristic grass-covered headquarters houses interesting galleries (including one on tropical swamps), a film theatre, a cafe and a viewing gallery. If you have binoculars then bring them; otherwise be prepared to wait to use the fixed points in the viewing galleries and hides. (香港濕地公園; ☑2708 8885; www.wetlandpark.gov.hk/en; Wetland Park Rd, Tin Shui Wai; adult/child HK$30/15; ☺10am-5pm Wed-Mon; ☒; ☒line 705 or 706)

Mai Po Nature Reserve
NATURE RESERVE

4 Map p130, C2

The 270-hectare nature reserve includes the Mai Po Visitor Centre at the northeastern end, where you must register; the Mai Po Education Centre to the south, with displays on the history and ecology of the wetland and Deep Bay; floating boardwalks and trails through the mangroves and mud flats; and a dozen hides (towers or huts from where you can watch birds up close without being observed). Disconcertingly, the cityscape of Shēnzhèn looms to the north. (米埔

自然保護區; ☑2471 3480; www.wwf.org.hk;
Mai Po, Sin Tin, Yuen Long; admission HK$120;
🕐9am-5pm; 🚌76K from Sheung Shui East
Rail or Yuen Long West Rail stations)

Ping Shan Heritage Trail

OUTDOORS

5 ◉ Map p130, B3

Hong Kong's first ever heritage trail
features historic buildings belonging to
the Tangs, the first and the most powerful of the 'Five Clans'. Highlights of the
1km trail include Hong Kong's oldest
pagoda (Tsui Sing Lau) a magnificent
ancestral hall, a temple, a study hall, a
well and a gallery inside an old police
station that was built by the British as
much to monitor the coastline as to
keep an eye on the clan. (屏山文物徑;
☑2617 1959; 🕐ancestral halls 9am-1pm &
2-5pm, Tsui Sing Lau 9am-1pm & 2-5pm, closed
Tue; Ⓜ West Rail Tin Shui Wai, exit E)

Sai Kung

VILLAGE

6 ◉ Map p130, H4

Apart from the Outlying Islands, the
Sai Kung Peninsula is one of the last
havens left in Hong Kong for hikers,
swimmers and boaters, and most of
it is one huge 7500-hectare country
park. A short journey to any of the
islands off Sai Kung town is rewarding. Hidden away are some excellent
beaches that can be visited by *kaido*
(small ferry boats), which depart from
the waterfront. The **MacLehose Trail**,
a 100km route across the New Territories, begins at Pak Tam Chung on
the Sai Kung Peninsula. On top of this,

Sai Kung town boasts superb Chinese
seafood restaurants, especially along
the attractive waterfront. (西貢; 🚌92,
Ⓜ Choi Hung, then minibus 1A or 1M, then bus
299; Ⓜ Sha Tin East Rail)

Eating

Chuen Kee Seafood Restaurant

SEAFOOD $$

Chuen Kee has two locations in Sai
Kung. This is the plush branch of the
flagship on the promenade (see 6 ◉
Map p130; H4). The elaborate display of
fish and crustaceans at the door may
make you cringe, but cringe will turn
to crave once you've had a bite of
the cooked versions. (全記海鮮菜館;
☑2792 6938; 87-89 Man Nin St; meals from
HK$180; 🕐7am-11pm; 🚌1)

Sam Shing Hui Seafood Market

SEAFOOD $$

7 Map p130, A4

Along Castle Peak Beach, this busy working seafood market sits adjacent to rows of *dai pai dong* (food stalls), as well as fancier enclosed establishments, ready to cook up whatever seafood you've picked. English is limited here, but pointing and smiling should get you going – just be sure to ask for prices first. (三聖墟海鮮市場; Sam Shing St, Castle Peak Bay, Tuen Mun; meals HK$150-300; ⏰10am-midnight; 🚌minibus 140M from Tsing Yi)

Tai Wing Wah

HAKKA $

8 Map p130, B3

The brainchild of celebrated chef Leung Man-to, Tai Wing Wah is most famous for its walled-village dishes. Leung sources local ingredients from small farms and food producers whenever possible. Must-eats include lemon-steamed grey mullet, smoked oysters and Malay sponge cake. (大榮華酒樓; 2nd fl, Koon Wong Mansion, 2-6 On Ning Rd; dim sum HK$16, dishes from HK$70; ⏰6am-midnight; 🚋Tai Tong Rd Light Rail station)

Anthony's Ranch

AMERICAN $$

The Disney-fied cowboy decor is goofy, but the excellently executed American-style burgers, ribs, pulled pork and apple pie are no joke (see 6 Map p130; H4). (📞2791 6113; www.anthonys-ranch. com; 28 Yi Chun St, Sai Kung; meals HK$150; ⏰11.30am-midnight Mon-Thu, to 2am Fri & Sat, from 8.30am Sun; 🚌1)

Yue Kee Roasted Goose Restaurant

CANTONESE $$

9 Map p130, C4

In an alley lined with roast-goose restaurants, 54-year-old Yue Kee is king. Try coppery-skinned charcoal-roasted goose (half is plenty for four people) and sample house specialities like soy-braised goose web (feet) or garlic-fried goose kidneys. There are also plenty of standard Cantonese dishes on offer. English menu. (裕記大飯店; 📞2491 0105; www.yuekee.com.hk/en; 9 Sham Hong Rd, Sham Tseng; meals HK$100-200; ⏰11am-11pm; 🚌minibus 302 from Tai Wo Hau MTR)

Sha Tin 18

CANTONESE $$

10 Map p130, G3

The Peking duck (whole HK$538, half HK$328) here has put this hotel restaurant, adjacent to the campus of the Chinese University, in the gastronomic spotlight since its opening in 2009. Book your duck 24 hours in advance, then try it in two ways – pancakes with the crispy skin, and wok-fried mince duck with iceberg lettuce. (沙田18; 📞3723 1234; www. hongkong.shatin.hyatt.com; 18 Chak Cheung St, Hyatt Regency Hong Kong; meals HK$300-500; ⏰11.30am-3pm & 5.30-10.30pm; Ⓜ University)

Honeymoon Dessert

DESSERTS $

This shop (see 6 Map p130; H4) specialises in Chinese desserts such as sweet walnut soup and durian pudding, and has branches all over China and in Indonesia. (滿記甜品; 📞2792 4991; 9, 10A, B&C Po Tung Rd; per person HK$30; ⏰1pm-2.45am; 🚌1)

Understand

Early Hong Kong

Hong Kong has supported human life since at least the Middle Neolithic Period (c 4000–2500 BC). Artefacts uncovered at almost 100 archaeological sites in the territory suggest the inhabitants of these settlements shared similar cultural characteristics to people living in the Pearl River Delta in China. The remnants of Bronze Age habitations (c 1500–220 BC) unearthed on Lamma and Lantau islands, and at around 20 other sites, also indicate that these early people practised some form of folk religion involving animal worship. Early Chinese historical records refer to the diverse maritime people in China's southeastern coastal area as the 'Hundred Yue' tribes. Some of the prehistoric inhabitants of Hong Kong might have belonged to these tribes.

The Five Great Clans

Hong Kong, along with the Yue tribes in Guǎngdōng, was incorporated into the Chinese empire during the Qin dynasty (c 221–206 BC). Archaeological finds in the following centuries showed that Hong Kong came under the influence of Han culture as more Han settlers migrated to the region. The discovery of coins and pottery from Eastern Han dynasty (AD 25–220) on Lantau and Kau Sai Chau islands, and at several important digs, including a tomb at Lei Cheng Uk in central Kowloon and So Kwun Wat southeast of Tuen Mun, attests to this.

The first of Hong Kong's mighty 'Five Clans' (all Han Chinese), whose descendants hold political and economic clout to this day, began settling the area around the 11th century. The first and most powerful of the arrivals were the Tang, who initially settled around Kam Tin (*tin* means 'field'). The Tang were followed by the Hau and the Pang, who spread around present-day Sheung Shui and Fanling. These were followed by the Liu in the 14th century and the Man a century later.

Punti Versus Tanka

The Cantonese-speaking newcomers called themselves *bun-day* (Punti), meaning 'indigenous' or 'local' – something they clearly were not. They looked down on the original inhabitants, the Tanka, many of whom had been shunted off the land and had moved onto the sea to live on boats.

Top Sights
Tian Tan Buddha

Getting There

⚓ **Ferry** Outlying Islands Terminal, Central Pier 6 to Mui Wo, Lantau Island

Ⓜ **MTR** Tung Chung

🚌 **Bus** 2 from Mui Wo, bus 23 from Tung Chung

At 23m (10 storeys), Tian Tan Buddha on Ngong Ping Plateau, Lantau Island, 500m above sea level, is the world's tallest seated bronze Buddha statue. In fact, 'Big Buddha' is so big you can see it on the plane flying into Hong Kong, and, on a clear day, from Macau. Hikers negotiating the slopes of Lantau are often caught off-guard by 'Big Buddha' looming suddenly into view like an idea in a stark blue sky, or shrouded in fog like an afterthought.

Tian Tan Buddha

Don't Miss

The Statue

Not many know this but the likeness of Lord Gautama was created by China Aerospace Science and Technology – the company that designs China's spaceships. The right hand is lifted in a gesture symbolic of a vow to eliminate suffering; the left is placed on the thigh, signifying compassion.

Exhibition Hall

The statue is reached by 268 steps. Inside the pedestal is an **exhibition hall** (☏2985 5248; ☺10am-6pm) containing oil paintings and ceramic plaques of the Buddha's life and teachings. The large computer-operated bell chimes 108 times during the day to symbolise escape from the '108 vexations of mankind'.

Po Lin Monastery

Eclipsed by the new buildings in front is the century-old **Po Lin Monastery** (寶蓮禪寺; ☏2985 5248; Lantau; ☺9am-6pm), founded here by three monks from Jiangsu province in 1906. There are temples, a tea garden and a restaurant.

Ngong Ping 360

The most spectacular way to reach the plateau is by the 5.7km **Ngong Ping 360** (昂平360纜車; adult/child/concession one way HK$86/44/70, return HK$125/62/98; ☺10am-6pm Mon-Fri, 9am-6.30pm Sat, Sun & public holidays), a cable car linking Ngong Ping with Tung Chung downhill. The journey over the bay and the mountains takes 25 minutes in glassed-in gondolas.

天壇大佛

admission free

☺10am-6pm

☑ Top Tips

▶ Unless you like cheesy multimedia shows, skip Ngong Ping Village where the cable car stops uphill.

▶ The restored **Old Tai O Police Station** (舊大澳警署: Tai O Heritage Hotel; ☏2985 8383; www.taioheritagehotel.com; Shek Tsai Po St; admission free; ☺tours 3pm & 4pm; ☐1 from Mui Wo, 11 from Tung Chung, 21 from Ngong Ping), c 1902, in Tai O, also on Lantau Island, has re-opened as the lovely Tai O Heritage Hotel. There's a free guided tour at 3pm and 4pm daily. Online reservation a must.

✕ Take a Break

Po Lin Vegetarian Restaurant (寶蓮禪寺齋堂; ☏2985 5248; Ngong Ping; set meals regular/deluxe HK$60/100; ☺11.30am-4.30pm) in the monastery offers cheap and filling vegetarian fare.

Local Life
Lamma Island

Getting There

⛴ **Ferry** Outlying Islands Terminal, Central: Pier 4. Most sailings stop at the larger village Yung Shue Wan; some stop at Sok Kwu Wan.

If Lamma had a soundtrack, it would be reggae. Hong Kong's most laidback outlying island attracts herb-growers, indie musicians and New Age therapists from a rainbow of cultures. Village stores stock Prosecco and Chinese mongrels obey commands in French. You can hike to the beach, your unlikely compass being three coal-fired plants against the skyline, looking more surreal than grim. Spend the afternoon chilling, and in the evening glow, feast on prawns and calamari by the pier.

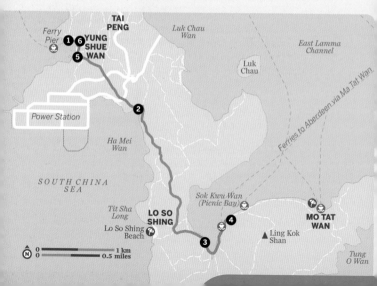

❶ Main Street, Yung Shue Wan

Spend a couple of hours exploring the shops in Yung Shue Wan (Banyan Bay). Plastic was the big industry here at one time, but now restaurants, bars and quaint little shops are the main employers. At the street's southern corner, there's a small **Tin Hau temple** founded in the late 19th century. You can stop for 'shepherdess' pie and thoughtfully crafted vegetarian delights at the granddad of Hong Kong's Western-style vegetarian eateries, **Bookworm Cafe** (南島書蟲; ☑2982 4838; 79 Main St, Yung Shue Wan; meals from HK$80; ☺9am-9pm Fri-Wed; ⛴Yung Shue Wan). Bookworm also doubles as a secondhand bookshop.

❷ Hung Shing Yeh Beach

All fuelled up with healthy yummies, begin the hour-long (4km) Family Trail that runs between Yung Shue Wan and Sok Kwu Wan. Lamma's most popular beach, Hung Shing Yeh, is located midway along the trail, and on weekdays it's almost deserted. The beach has toilets and changing rooms, and there are drinks stands nearby that are open on the weekend. You can also stock up on cold cuts and wine while in the village, for an impromptu picnic.

❸ Kamikaze Caves

At idyllic Sok Kwu Wan (Picnic Bay, but literally, 'strings and fishnets bay'), there are three 'kamikaze caves': grottoes built by the Japanese to house explosives-wired motorboats to be deployed – or so the story goes – on suicide missions during WWII.

❹ Sok Kwu Wan

Also at Sok Kwu Wan, there's **Lamma Fisherfolk's Village** (漁民文化村; ☑2982 8585; lammafisherfolks.com.hk; adult/child HK$60/50; ☺10am-7pm Mon-Fri), a floating museum and theme park that showcases Hong Kong's fishing culture, and a renovated **Tin Hau temple** (天后廟), c 1826.

❺ Lamcombe Seafood Restaurant

Hike back to Yung Shue Wan for dinner. **Lamcombe** (☑2982 0881; 47 Main St; meals from HK$120; ☺11am-2.30pm, 5-10pm) has been serving up tasty fried squid and steamed scallops for over 10 years. Portions are big and service is decent.

❻ Island Bar

Need one for the road? This **bar** (☺5pm-late Mon-Fri, noon-late Sat & Sun, happy hour 5-8pm; ⛴Yung Shue Wan) is the closest one to the ferry pier and the oldest watering hole on Lamma. Long-term expats come here for the low-down on everything. It's also the home of the feisty Lamma ladies' dragon-boat team.

Explore

Trip to Macau

China's Special Administrative Region (SAR) of Macau may be known as the Vegas of the East, but the city has much more to offer than casinos. There are fortresses, churches and neighbourhoods that evoke the style of its former Portuguese masters, intermixed with Chinese temples and shrines. And of course, no trip to Macau is complete without tasting Macanese food, a delicious celebration of hybridism.

The Sights in a Day

Spend 90 minutes at the **Ruins of the Church of St Paul** (p142), its small museum, and the nearby **Macau Museum** (p149). Wander southwest through the tiny streets towards the Inner Harbour, stopping at the **Mandarin's House** (p150), **St Joseph's Seminary & Church** (p143) and **A-Ma Temple** (p148). Have lunch at **Alfonso III** (p151), then cab it north to the lovely **St Lazarus Church District** (p150) to browse the boutiques and art spaces for a while.

After lunch, head up to **Guia Fort** (p148) for a visit to the tiny but gorgeous Chapel of Our Lady of Guia. Don't miss the lighthouse and the panoramic views of the city. Then, if you like, pay a visit to the magnificent **Kun Iam Temple** (p148).

Have dinner at **A Petisqueira** (p151) in Taipa. Make your way back to Macau Peninsula for drinks and live music at **Macau Soul** (p154). Alternatively, spend some time checking out and drinking at one of the city's many casinos.

For a local's day exploring Taipa and Coloane Islands, see p144.

 Top Sights

Ruins of the Church of St Paul (p142)

Local Life

Exploring Taipa & Coloane Islands (p144)

Best of Macau

Eating

António (p151)

A Petisqueira (p151)

Clube Militar de Macau (p151)

Drinking

Macallan Whisky Bar & Lounge (p153)

Macau Soul (p154)

Getting There

🚢 **Ferry** Catch the **TurboJet** (☑ bookings 852-2921 6688, in Hong Kong 790 7039, information 852-2859 3333; www.turbojet.com.hk; economy/superclass Mon-Fri HK\$142/244, Sat & Sun HK\$154/260, night crossing HK\$176/275) from the **Hong Kong–Macau Ferry Terminal** (Shun Tak Centre, 200 Connaught Rd, Sheung Wan) or the **China Ferry Terminal** (中港碼頭; China Hong Kong City, 33 Canton Rd, Tsim Sha Tsui). Both trips take about an hour.

Top Sights
Ruins of the Church of St Paul

Essentially a magnificent gate to nowhere, the ruins of the Church of St Paul are Macau's most treasured icon. Once part of a Jesuit church, it was designed by an Italian Jesuit and built by exiled Japanese Christians and Chinese craftsmen in 1602. However, due to a fire in 1835, all that remain are a weathered facade and a majestic stairway. Yet with surviving statues and engravings making up what some call a 'sermon in stone', it's still considered one of the greatest monuments to Christianity in Asia.

◉ Map p146, B2

大三巴牌坊, Ruinas de Igreja de São Paulo

Travessa de São Paulo

admission free

🚌8A, 17, 26, disembark at Luís de Camões Garden

Ruins of the Church of St Paul

Don't Miss

Asian Details

The Christian facade is full of Asian details. On the third tier stands the Virgin Mary being assumed into heaven along with angels and two flowers: the peony, representing China, and the chrysanthemum, a symbol of Japan. To her right is a carving of the apocalyptic woman (Mary) slaying a seven-headed hydra; the Japanese kanji reads: 'The holy mother tramples the heads of the dragon'.

Museum of Sacred Art

This small **museum** (天主教藝術博物館和墓室, Museu de Arte Sacra e Cripta; Rua de São Paulo; admission free; ☺9am-6pm; ☒8A, 17, 26, disembark at Luís de Camões Garden) contains polychrome carved wooden statues, silver chalices and oil paintings, including a copy of a 17th-century painting depicting the martyrdom of Japanese Christians by crucifixion at Nagasaki in 1597. The adjoining crypt contains the remains of Asian Christian martyrs and the tomb of Alessandro Valignano, who's credited with establishing Christianity in Japan.

Nearby: Churches

With a scalloped entrance canopy (European), a roof of beams and rafters (Chinese) and China's oldest dome, **St Joseph's Seminary & Church** (聖若瑟修院及聖堂, Capela do Seminario Sao Jose; Rua do Seminario; ☺church 10am-5pm; ☒9, 16, 18, 28B), built 1746 to 1758, is Macau's most beautiful example of tropicalised baroque architecture. The 17th-century baroque **Church of St Dominic** (玫瑰堂, Igreja de São Domingos; Largo de São Domingos; ☺10am-6pm; ☒3, 6, 26A) has a fine altar and ecclesiastical art in its treasury.

☑ **Top Tips**

▸ To beat the crowds, get to the facade before 9am, then visit the museum as soon as it opens.

✗ **Take a Break**

The streets nearby are littered with shops selling almond cookies and pork jerky.

Local Life
Exploring Taipa & Coloane Islands

Taipa was created from two islands joined together by silt from the Pearl River. Land reclamation has succeeded in doing the same thing to Taipa and Coloane, now joined by the Cotai Strip, 'Cotai' being a portmanteau of Coloane and Taipa. Scenic Taipa has rapidly urbanised, though you'll still find old shops alongside delicious Macanese eateries. The small island of Coloane was once a haven for pirates but today largely retains Macau's old way of life.

① Taipa Village
Take bus 22, 26 or 33 to get to this village in the south of the island, where the historical part of Taipa is best preserved. With a tidy sprawl of traditional Chinese shops and some excellent restaurants, the village is punctuated by grand colonial villas, churches and

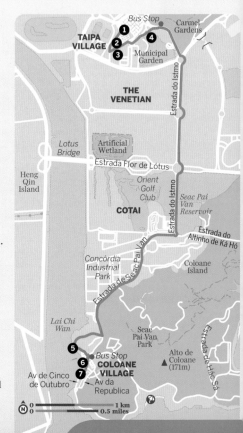

ancient temples. Avenida da Praia, a tree-lined esplanade with wrought-iron benches, is perfect for a leisurely stroll.

❷ Pak Tai Temple

Sitting quietly in a leafy square in the village is this **temple** (Rua do Regedor; 🚌22, 28A, 26), built in 1844 and dedicated to the Taoist god of the north. A pair of Chinese lions guards the entrance to the temple.

❸ Museum of Taipa & Coloane History

This **museum** (路氹歷史館, Museu da História da Taipa e Coloane; 📞2882 5361; Rua Correia da Silva, Taipa; adult/student MOP$5/2, child & senior free, Tue free; ⏰10am-5.30pm Tue-Sun; 🚌11, 15, 22, 28A, 30, 33, 34) has a display of excavated relics and other artefacts on the 1st floor, while the 2nd floor contains religious objects, handicrafts and architectural models.

❹ Taipa House Museum

Further afield, the pastel-toned **villas** (龍環葡韻住宅式博物館, Casa Museum da Taipa; 📞2882 7103; Avenida da Praia, Carmo Zone, Taipa; adult/student MOP$5/2, child & senior free, Sun free; ⏰10am-5.30pm Tue-Sun; 🚌11, 15, 22, 28A, 30, 33, 34) here were once the summer residences of middle-class Macanese; now they're museums showcasing Portuguese traditions, Macau's traditional industries and local life in the early 20th century.

❺ Stilt Houses

Head to Coloane by bus 21A from the bus stop on Estrada Governador Nobre de Carvalho, and alight at Coloane Village. On **Rua Dos Navegantes** in Coloane's old fishing village, there are a few old stilt houses of colourful corrugated metal that were once landing spots for house boats. You'll see them near Largo do Cais, the square just off the old pier of Coloane. From the square, take the slope to the right of the Servicos de Alfangega building. After two minutes, you'll see the cavernous cadaver of a shipyard, also on stilts.

❻ Chapel of St Francis Xavier

The highlight here is this quirky **chapel** (聖方濟各教堂, Capela de São Francisco Xavier; Rua do Caetano, Largo Eduardo Marques, Coloane; ⏰10am-8pm; 🚌15, 21A, 25, 26A), built in 1928, which contains paintings of the infant Christ with a Chinese Madonna, as well as other interesting artefacts of Christianity and colonialism in Asia.

❼ Temples

Southeast of the chapel, between Travessa de Caetano and Travessa de Pagode, is a dainty **Kun Iam Temple**, a mere altar inside a walled compound. A little further to the southeast, there's a **Tin Hau Temple** (天后廟) on Avenida da Republica up in Largo Tin Hau Miu. At the south end of Avenida de Cinco de Outubro, Taoist **Tam Kong Temple** (譚公廟; Avenida de Cinco de Outubro, Largo Tam Kong Miu; ⏰8.30am-5.30pm; 🚌15, 21A, 25, 26A) has a model of a dragon boat made from whalebone.

SOUTH CHINA SEA

Av Norte da Amizade

Outer Harbour Ferry Terminal

Fisherman's Wharf

2 Macau Museum of Art

Avenida Xian Xing Hai

Rua dos Pescadores

Cemetery

Reservoir

Av do Nordeste

8 AFA (Art for All Society)

Av do Coronel Mesquita

4 Kun Iam Temple

Av do Conselheiro Ferreira de Almeida

Guia Hill

Guia Fort & Guia Chapel **3**

Avenida da Amizade

Rua de Luís Gonzaga Gomes

Avenida de Paris

Rua de Lisboa

NAPE

Av do Dr Sun Yat Sen

Estrada da Areia Preta

Av Horta e Costa

Lou Lim Ioc Garden

Estrada do Cemitério

23

St Lazarus Church District

Av do Dr Rodrigo

Avenida de Lisboa

Jardim des Artes

Inner Harbour

Rua da Ribeira do Patane

Luís de Camões Garden & Grotto

Rotunda de Carlos da Maia

Monte Fort

19 **5**

Ruins of the Church of St Paul

Travessa de São Paulo

Largo de São Domingos

9 **9**

Lou Kau Mansion **6**

14

20

12 Ponte Governador Nobre de Carvalho

Qiamshan Waterway

Rua do Almirante Sérgio

Av de Almeida Ribeiro

Rua Central

Largo de St Agostinho

11 New Yaohan

Stanley Ho Site

Mandarin's House **7**

Baía da Praia (Lagos de Nam Van)

Avenida Doutor Stanley Ho

Rua da Barra

Penha Hill

A-Ma Temple **1**

Rua de São Tiago da Barra

Lago Sai Van

Av da República

Av Dr Sun Yat Sen

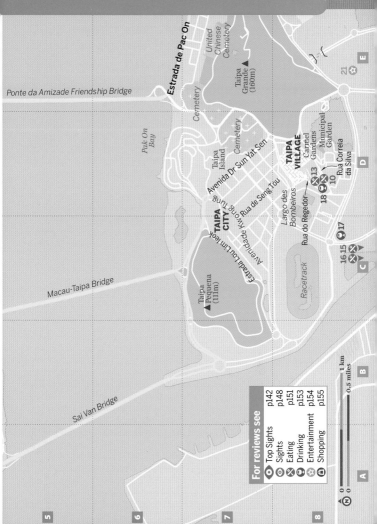

Ponte da Amizade Friendship Bridge

Estrada de Pac On

United Chinese Cemetery

Cemetery

▲ Taipa Grande (160m)

E

Cemetery

Pak On Bay

Cemetery

Taipa Island

Avenida Dr Sun Yat Sen

Rua de Seng Tou

TAIPA VILLAGE

Carmel Gardens

Municipal Garden

21 ⊕ ✦

Rua Correia da Silva

D

TAIPA CITY

Avenida Kwong Tung

Largo des Bombeiros

⊗13 ⊗
⊗ 10
18 ⊗

Rua do Regedor

16 15 ⊗ ⊗
⊗ 17

C

Estrada Lou Lim Ieok

▲ Taipa Pequena (111m)

Macau-Taipa Bridge

Racetrack

Sai Van Bridge

For reviews see	
◉ Top Sights	p142
◉ Sights	p148
⊗ Eating	p151
◐ Drinking	p153
✦ Entertainment	p154
🛍 Shopping	p155

0 ___ 1 km
0 ___ 0.5 miles

Ⓝ

A B

5

6

7

8

Sights

A-Ma Temple TEMPLE

1 ◉ Map p146, A4

A-Ma Temple was probably already standing when the Portuguese arrived, although the present structure may date from the 16th century. It was here that fisherfolk once came to replenish supplies and pray for fair weather. A-Ma, aka Tin Hau, is the goddess of the sea, from which the name Macau is derived. It's believed that when the Portuguese asked for the name of the place, they were told 'A-Ma Gau' (A-Ma Bay). In modern Cantonese, 'Macau' (Ou Mun) means 'gateway of the bay'. (媽閣廟, Templo de A-Ma; Rua de São Tiago da Barra; ⏰7am-6pm; 🚌1, 2, 5, 6B, 7)

Macau Museum of Art MUSEUM

2 ◉ Map p146, D3

This excellent five-storey museum has well-curated displays of art created in Macau and China, including paintings by Western artists like George Chinnery, who lived in the enclave. Other highlights are ceramics and stoneware excavated in Macau, Ming- and Qing-dynasty calligraphy from Guǎngdōng, ceramic statues from Shíwān (Guǎngdōng) and seal carvings. The museum also features 19th-century Western historical paintings from all over Asia, and contemporary Macanese art. (澳門藝術博物館, Museu de Arte de Macau; ☎8791 9814; www. mam.gov.mo; Macau Cultural Centre, Avenida Xian Xing Hai; adult/child MOP$5/2, Sun free; ⏰10am-6.30pm Tue-Sun; 🚌1A, 8, 12, 23)

Guia Fort & Guia Chapel FORT, CHURCH

3 ◉ Map p146, C2

As the highest point on the peninsula, Guia Fort affords panoramic views of the city and, when the air is clear, across to the islands and China. At the top is the stunning Chapel of Our Lady of Guia built in 1622 and retaining almost 100% of its original features, including some of Asia's most valuable frescoes. Next to it stands the oldest modern **lighthouse** on the China coast – an attractive 15m-tall structure that is closed to the public. (東望洋炮台及聖母雪地殿聖堂, Fortaleza da Guia e Capela de Guia; ⏰chapel 9am-5.30pm; 🚌2, 2A, 6A, 12, 17, 18 Flora Garden stop)

Kun Iam Temple TEMPLE

4 ◉ Map p146, C1

Macau's oldest temple was founded in the 13th century, but the present structures date back to 1627. Its roofs are embellished with porcelain figurines and its halls are lavishly decorated. Inside the main one stands the likeness of Kun Iam, the Goddess of Mercy; to the left of the altar is a statue of a bearded arhat rumoured to represent Marco Polo. The first Sino-American treaty was signed at a round stone table in the temple's terraced gardens in 1844. (觀音廟, Templo de Kun Iam; 2 Avenida do Coronel Mesquita; ⏰7am-5.30pm; 🚌1A, 10, 18A, stop Travessa de Venceslau de Morais)

MEGAN EAVES/LONELY PLANET ©

A-Ma Temple

Monte Fort

FORT

5  Map p146, B2

Just east of the ruins, Monte Fort was built by the Jesuits between 1617 and 1626 as part of the College of the Mother of God. Barracks and storehouses were designed to allow the fort to survive a two-year siege, but the cannons were fired only once, during the aborted attempt by the Dutch to invade Macau in 1622. Now the ones on the south side are trained at the gaudy Grand Lisboa Casino like an accusing finger. (大炮台, Fortaleza do Monte; ⏰7am-7pm; 🚍7, 8, disembark at Social Welfare Bureau)

Macau Museum

MUSEUM

This interesting museum inside Monte Fort (see 5  Map p146; B2) will give you a taste of Macau's history. The 1st floor introduces the territory's early history and includes an elaborate section on Macau's religions. Highlights of the 2nd floor include a recreated firecracker factory and a recorded reading in the local dialect by Macanese poet José dos Santos Ferreira (1919–93). The top floor focuses on new architecture and urban-development plans. (澳門博物館, Museu de Macau; 📞2835 7911; www. macaumuseum.gov.mo; 112 Praceta do Museu de Macau; admission MOP$15, 15th of month free; ⏰10am-5.30pm Tue-Sun; 🚌7, 8, disembark at Social Welfare Bureau)

Lou Kau Mansion   HISTORIC BUILDING

6 ◉ Map p146, B3

Built around 1889, this Cantonese-style mansion with southern European elements belonged to merchant Lou Wa Sio (aka Lou Kau), who also commissioned the **Lou Lim Ioc Garden** (盧廉若公園, Jardim Lou Lim Ieoc; 10 Estrada de Adolfo de Loureiro; ⏰6am-9pm; 🚌2, 2A, 5, 9, 9A, 12, 16). Behind the grey facade, an intriguing maze of open and semi-enclosed spaces blurs the line between inside and outside. The flower-and-bird motif on the roof can also be found in the Mandarin's House and A-Ma Temple. Free guided tours in Chinese on weekends (from 10am to 7pm). (盧家大屋, Casa de Lou Kau; ☎8399 6699; 7 Travessa da Sé; admission free; ⏰10am-5.30pm Tue-Sun; 🚌3, 4, 6A, 8A, 19, 33)

Mandarin's House   HISTORIC BUILDING

7 ◉ Map p146, A3

Built around 1869, the Mandarin's House with over 60 rooms, was the ancestral home of Zheng Guanying, an influential author-merchant whose readers had included emperors, Dr Sun Yat-sen and Chairman Mao. The compound features a moon gate, tranquil courtyards, exquisite rooms and a main hall with French windows, all arranged in that labyrinthine style typical of certain Chinese period buildings. (鄭家大屋, Caso do Mandarim; ☎2896 8820; www.wh.mo/man-darinhouse; 10 Travessa de Antonio da Silva; admission free; ⏰10am-5.30pm Thu-Tue; 🚌28B, 18)

AFA (Art for All Society)   GALLERY

8 ◉ Map p146, C1

Macau's best contemporary art can be seen at this nonprofit gallery, which has taken Macau's art worldwide and holds monthly solo exhibitions by Macau's top artists. AFA is near the **Mong Há Multi-Sport Pavilion** (望廈體育館). Disembark from the bus at Rua da Barca or Rua de Francisco Xavier Pereira. Alternatively, it's a 20-minute walk from Largo do Senado. (全藝社; ☎2836 6064; www.afamacau.com; 3rd fl, Edificio da Fabrica de Baterias N E National, 52 Estrada da Areia Preta; ⏰noon-7pm Mon-Sat; 🚌8, 8A, 18A, 7)

St Lazarus Church District   NEIGHBOURHOOD

9 ◉ Map p146, B2

A lovely neighbourhood with colonial-style houses and cobbled streets. Designers and independents like to gather here, setting up shop and organising artsy events, such as the weekly **Sun Never Left – Public Art Performance** (黃昏小叙-街頭藝術表演; www.cipa.org.mo; Rua de Sao Roque; ⏰3-6pm Sat & Sun; 🚌7, 8). **Tai Fung Tong Art House** (大瘋堂藝舍; ☎2835 3537; 7 Calcada de Sao Lazaro; ⏰2-6pm Tue-Sun; 🚌7, 8), **G32** (☎2834 6626; 32 Rua de Sao Miguel; ⏰free guided tours 2.30-5pm Sat & Sun; 🚌7, 8), and the Old Ladies' House are also here. (瘋堂斜巷, Calcada da Igreja de Sao Lazaro; www.cipa.org.mo; 🚌7, 8)

Eating

António
PORTUGUESE $$$

 10 Map p146, D8

The cosy mahogany-framed dining room, the meticulously thought-out menu and the entertaining chef, António Coelho, all make this the go-to place for traditional Portuguese food. If you can only try one Portuguese restaurant in Macau, make it this one. (安東尼奧; ☑2899 9998; www.antoniomacau.com; 7 Rua dos Clerigos, Taipa; meals MOP$350-1200; ⏰noon-10.30pm; ☒22, 26)

Alfonso III
PORTUGUESE $$

11 Map p146, B3

A short stroll southwest of Leal Senado is this tiny, family-run restaurant that has won a well-deserved reputation among Macau's Portuguese community. Service is patchy, but no one seems to mind. Tables are often in short supply, so phone ahead. (亞豐素三世餐廳; ☑2858 6272; 11a Rua Central; meals MOP$300; ⏰11.30am-2.30pm & 6-9.30pm; 👶; ☒3, 6, 26A)

Guincho a Galera
PORTUGUESE $$$

12 Map p146, B3

The international branch of Portugal's famous Fortaleza do Guincho, this luxuriously decorated restaurant brings Portuguese haute cuisine to Macau. The menu features well-executed classical dishes, with a couple of Macanese additions.

Top Tip

Casino Shuttles

All big-name casinos have free shuttle services to and from the ferry terminals, the border gate into mainland China and the airport. Anyone can use these buses no questions asked (some rides even come with free chips!). You'll see them outside the ferry terminals and the casinos. For border gate and airport routes, enquire at the casinos.

Set meals are available at lunch (from MOP$300) and dinner (from MOP$600). (葡国餐廳; ☑8803 7676; 3rd fl, Hotel Lisboa, 2-4 Avenida de Lisboa; meals MOP$550-1800; ⏰noon-2.30pm & 6.30-10.30pm; ☒3, 10)

A Petisqueira
PORTUGUESE $

13 Map p146, D8

'The Snackery' is an amicable place with myriad Portuguese choices set in an obscure alley. It serves its own *queijo fresca da casa* (homemade cheese). Try the bacalao five ways, and baked seafood with rice. (葡國美食天地; ☑2882 5354; 15 Rua de São João, Taipa; meals MOP$150-500; ⏰12.30-2.15pm & 6.45-10pm Tue-Sun; 👶; ☒22, 28A)

Clube Militar
de Macau
PORTUGUESE $$

14 Map p146, B3

Housed in a distinguished colonial building, with fans spinning lazily

Understand
Mediterrasian Macau

The Portuguese colonisation of Macau, which lasted from the mid-16th century to 1999, left a legacy of southern European–style buildings in the Chinese city. But what appears to be Portuguese architecture is often a complex fusion of Portuguese and Chinese building styles, techniques and materials, with influences from Goa (India), the Philippines and Malacca (Malaysia) – as well as contributions from the Italian and Spanish missionaries who enriched it with their sensibilities and traditions. Generally, the only buildings that are entirely Chinese or Portuguese are, respectively, temples and fortresses.

Churches
Macau's churches feature a baroque style simplified and adapted for the tropical climate, similar to that found in Goa and Brazil. A characteristic of this tropicalised baroque architecture is the use of wood in place of stone – the Chinese were experts at carpentry, while the southern Europeans were master masons.

You can see this at St Joseph's Seminary & Church (p143), one of Macau's most beautiful buildings. Consecrated in 1758, it has a lemon-meringue facade, a scalloped canopy at the entrance and the first dome to be built in all of China. Inside, you'll find decorations made of plaster – common in this part of the world – and a timber roof propped up by a Chinese system of triangular beams and rafters, and covered with Guǎngdōng tiles attached by cement for protection against tropical monsoons.

The Church of St Dominic (p143) has light wooden balconies and wide-open windows, both characteristics of a hot climate.

Residences
The Mandarin's House (p150), a Qing-dynasty southern Chinese residential complex, has Western-style arches and window panels inlaid with mother-of-pearl, a technique of ornamentation also practised in India, the Philippines and Turkey.

above, the Military Club takes you back in time to a slower and quieter Macau. The simple and delicious Portuguese fare is complemented by an excellent selection of wine and cheese from Portugal. The MOP$153 buffet is excellent value. Reservations are required for dinner and weekend lunches. (陸軍俱樂部; ☎2871 4000; www.clubemilitardemacau.net; 975 Avenida da Praia Grande; meals MOP$150-400; ⏱1.45-2.30pm & 7-10.30pm Mon-Fri, noon-2.30pm & 7-10pm Sat & Sun; ◻6, 28C)

Café Nga Tim
MACANESE $

15 Map p146, C8

We love the Chinese-Portuguese food, the small-town atmosphere, the view of the Chapel of St Francis Xavier, the prices and the owner – a guitar- and *erhu*-strumming ex-policeman named Feeling Wong. (雅憩花園餐廳; Rua do Caetano, Coloane; mains MOP$70-200; ⏱noon-1am; 👶; ◻21A, 25, 26A)

Lord Stow's Bakery
BAKERY $

16 Map p146, C8

Though the celebrated English baker Andrew Stow passed away, his cafe (9 Largo do Matadouro) and Lord Stow's Bakery keep his memory well alive by serving his renowned *pastéis de nata*, a warm egg-custard tart (MOP$8), and cheesecake (MOP$14) in unusual flavours, including black sesame and green tea. (澳門安德魯餅店; 1 Rua da Tassara; ⏱7am-10pm Thu-Tue, to 7pm Wed)

Lord Stow's Bakery

Drinking

Macallan Whisky Bar & Lounge
BAR

17 Map p146, C8

Macau's best whisky bar is a traditional affair featuring oak panels, Jacobean rugs and a real fireplace. The 400-plus whisky labels include representatives from Ireland, France, Sweden and India, and a 1963 Glenmorangie. (☎8883 2221; www.galaxymacau.com; 203, 2nd fl, Galaxy Hotel, Cotai; ⏱5pm-1am Mon-Thu, to 2am Fri & Sat; ◻25, 25X)

MEGAN EAVES/LONELY PLANET ©

Local Life

Macau's Sword Master

The charismatic **Antonio Conceição Junior** (www.arscives.com/bladedesign) is Macau's best-known designer. He has a vast repertoire, spanning postage stamps, fashion, jewellery and book covers.

Antonio also designs custom swords inspired by Macanese and ancient cultures, mythology and the modern world – both Eastern (*katana* and *tantō*) and Western (sabres and cutlasses) blades, as well as hybrids.

Antonio can recommend blade-smiths in North America to manu-facture and ship the swords. Email him for enquiries; expect about one to two weeks for the completed de-sign and a fee of about US$3000.

Old Taipa Tavern

PUB

18 Map p146, D8

A location near the Pak Tai Temple makes laid-back OTT a sublime spot to watch the comings and goings in the centre of Taipa village. (好客鄉村餐廳; 21 Rua dos Negociantes, Taipa; 🛜; 🚌22, 28A, 26)

Macau Soul

BAR

19 Map p146, B2

An elegant haven in wood and stained glass, where twice a month, a jazz band plays to a packed audience. On most nights though, Thelonious Monk fills the air as customers chat with the owners and dither over their 430 Portuguese wines. Opening hours vary; phone ahead. (澳感廊; 📞2836 5182; www.macausoul.com; 31a Rua de São Paulo; ⏱3-10pm Sun, Mon & Thu, to midnight Fri & Sat; 🚌8A, 17, 26)

Entertainment

Grand Lisboa Casino

CASINO

20 ⭐ Map p146, B3

The only Macau-born casino, the plush Grand Lisboa, with its glowing bulb exterior and flaming-torch-shaped tower, has become the land-mark by which people navigate the peninsula's streets. (新葡京; 📞2838 2828; Avenida de Lisboa, Macau Peninsula; 🚌3, 10)

House of Dancing Water

THEATRE

21 ⭐ Map p146, E8

'The House of Dancing Water', Macau's most expensively made show, is a breathtaking melange of stunts, acrobatics and theatre designed by Franco Dragone, the former direc-tor of Cirque du Soleil. The magic revolves around a cobalt pool the size of several Olympic-sized swimming pools, over, around, into and under which a cast of 80 perform hair-raising stunts dressed in glorious costumes. (水舞間; 📞8868 6688; http://thehouseofdancingwater.com; City of Dreams, Estrada do Istmo, Cotai; tickets MOP$580-980; 🚌50, 35)

Mercearia Portuguesa

Live Music Association LIVE MUSIC

22 ⭐ Map p146, C1

The go-to place for indie music in Macau, this excellent dive inside an industrial building has hosted local and overseas acts, including Cold Cave, Buddhistson, Mio Myo and Pet Conspiracy. See the website for what's on. Macau indie bands to watch out for include WhyOceans (www.why-oceans.com) and Turtle Giant (www.turtlegiant.com). (LMA; 現場音樂協會; www.lmamacau.com; 11b San Mei Industrial Bldg, 50 Avenida do Coronel Mesquita; 🚌3, 9, 32, 12, 25)

Shopping

Mercearia Portuguesa FOOD

23 🔒 Map p146, B2

The charming Portuguese corner shop opened by a film director and actress has a small but well-curated selection of provisions, which includes honey, faience, wooden toys and jewellery from Portugal, gorgeously packaged and reasonably priced. (📞2856 2708; www.merceariaportuguesa.com; 8 Calçada da Igreja de São Lázaro; 🕐1-8pm Mon-Fri, noon-8pm Sat & Sun; 🚌7, 8)

The Best of
Hong Kong

Stall outside Sik Sik Yuen Wong Tai Sin Temple (p124)
RICHARD I'ANSON/GETTY IMAGES ©

Best Walks
Postwar Buildings & Colonial Life in Tsim Sha Tsui

🏃 The Walk

In early colonial days, Tsim Sha Tsui (TST) was a garden city inhabited by Europeans. Nathan Rd was lined by colonial houses and Chinese banyans were planted to provide shade. Chinese weren't allowed to live in TST until the early 20th century when the area was being developed into a trade hub. After the communist takeover in 1949, many Shanghainese businessmen fled to Hong Kong; some settled in TST. In the northern part of the district are postwar buildings that were once homes to this Chinese ethnic group.

Start Former Kowloon British School; Ⓜ Tsim Sha Tsui, exit B1

Finish Jordan Path; Ⓜ Jordan, exit A

Length 2.5km; two hours

✖ Take a Break

Chicken HOF & Soju Korean (李家; Kimberley Rd, G/F, 84 Kam Kok Mansion, Tsim Sha Tsui; meals from HK$150; ⏰ 5pm-4am; Ⓜ Jordan, exit D) On the way to Chatham Rd South from Austin Ave.

St Andrew's Anglican Church (p99)

❶ Former Kowloon British School

To reach this former school, turn right from exit B1 of Tsim Sha Tsui MTR station and walk north along Nathan Rd. Next door is **St Andrew's Anglican Church** (p99), Kowloon's oldest Anglican church. Further north on Nathan Rd, turn right into Austin Rd, a former stronghold of Shanghainese migrants.

❷ Pak On Building

Explore **Pak On Building** (百安大廈) with its lobby arcade littered with shops, including, down near Tak Shing St, a liquor store that stocks absinthe. Further down, where Austin Rd branches into Austin Ave, there's a late-1960s building with rounded balconies spiralling skyward.

❸ Carnival Mansion

Carnival Mansion (嘉華大廈) has a courtyard where you can stare up at a vortex of rickety postwar homes. Inside are yellow terrazzo stairs with green balustrades made by Shanghainese craftsmen half a century ago.

4 Success Stationery

Next door is **Success** (成功文具行) stationery shop, run by Ray and Philip since the '70s. You'll also spot the curious **triangular public toilet** (三角公廁). Continue down Austin Ave and make a left on Chatham Rd South. **Rosary Church** (玫瑰堂) is Kowloon's oldest Catholic church.

5 Gun Club Hill Barracks

At the big junction, make a left into Austin Rd. The cannon-guarded gates of **Gun Club Hill Barracks** (槍會山軍營), now home to the People's Liberation Army (PLA), is on its other side. Turn into the leafy alley (Jordan Path) just next to the gates.

6 Jordan Path

Note how functional buildings loom up

on your right, while manicured lawns of colonial recreation clubs unfurl on your left. As you near Jordan Rd, you'll see **PLA hospital** (解放軍駐軍醫院) with its darkened windows. Crossing Cox's Rd will take you to the Victorian-style, Anglican **Kowloon Union Church** (c 1927; 九龍佑寧堂). Continue along Jordan Rd for Jordan MTR station.

Best Walks
Wan Chai's Forgotten Streets

🏃 The Walk

Wan Chai's coastline used to run near the tram tracks on Johnston Rd before zealous land reclamation pushed the shoreline to the north. During that time, the area around Queen's Rd East and Johnston Rd was a fishing village with shrines and temples overlooking the sea. After the British came, shipyards were built along the bay and 'second-rank' Europeans who could not afford to live on Victoria Peak made their homes on the hills south of Queen's Rd East. Though new Wan Chai is an exciting commercial district with gleaming skyscrapers and five-star hotels, for those keen on exploration, the south side of the (tram) tracks will always be more interesting.

Start Pak Tai Temple; Ⓜ Wan Chai, exit A3

Finish Star St; Ⓜ Admiralty, exit F

Length 1.2km; two hours

✕ Take a Break

La Creperie (100 Queen's Rd E, 1st fl, Wan Chai; meals HK$70-200; 🕙 11.30am-11pm Mon-Sun; Ⓜ Wan Chai, exit A3)

Roof detail, Pak Tai Temple (p72)

RELIGIOUS IMAGES/UIG/GETTY IMAGES ©

❶ Pak Tai Temple

A five-minute stroll south from Wan Chai MTR station, past Johnston Rd, lies stunning **Pak Tai Temple** (p72), built 150 years ago by local residents.

❷ Hong Kong House of Stories

Further down the slope on Stone Nullah Lane, the **Hong Kong House of Stories** (p73), aka the Blue House, will show you what life was like in Wan Chai in the last century (the house has no toilet-flushing facilities). It was painted blue during a renovation in the 1920s because the government had surplus blue paint.

❸ Old Wan Chai Post Office

Head west on Queen's Rd East and glance across at the **streamline moderne facade** of a shopping centre that used to be the Wan Chai Market. Once the neighbourhood hub, the market was used as a mortuary by Japanese forces in WWII. The pocket-sized **Old Wan Chai Post Office** (p73) is Hong Kong's oldest.

❹ Spring Garden Lane

Cross the road to take a look at Spring Garden Lane, one of the first areas developed by the British. A British merchant had a lavish residence here named Spring Gardens, and Spring Garden Lane was the length between its north and south gates. In the 1900s the lane harboured many brothels.

❺ Ghost House

Come back to the southern side of Queen's Rd East. Peep inside mysterious **Hung Shing Temple** (p72), once a seaside shrine. Just west of the temple turn up the hill along Ship St and stand before the now-derelict **Ghost House** at 55 Nam Koo Terrace. Its history is a wretched one: it was used by Japanese soldiers as a brothel housing 'comfort women' in WWII.

❻ Star Street

Star St neighbourhood is a quiet corner that contains the old – including a family-run *dai pai dong* (hawker-style food stall) on St Francis St – and the new, such as quaint boutiques, cafes and restaurants. Just above **Classified** (p79) is a six-storey balconied building in art-deco style. At the junction of Wing Fung St and Queen's Rd East you'll see a building with signage to the Admiralty MTR station just under it.

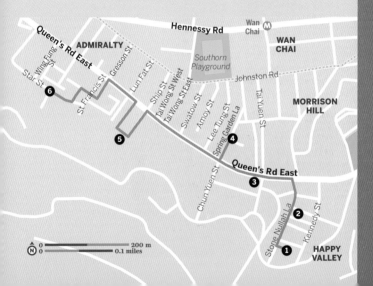

Best Walks
Wholesale District (Sheung Wan)

🏃 The Walk

Sheung Wan became a trading hub in the mid-19th century, when turmoil in China caused Chinese businessmen to flee to the territory. They set up businesses in Sheung Wan, trading in dried seafood, herbs and rice. Not everyone who arrived was rich, though. The majority worked as coolies at the piers. As more migrants came, the area around Tai Ping Shan St became the heart of the Chinese community, with its own temples and funeral parlours. Sheung Wan was also tied to Dr Sun Yat-sen, who went to school here and, later, held secret meetings as a revolutionary.

Start Kennedy Town tram (Sutherland St stop)

Finish 🚌26, Hollywood Rd; Ⓜ Sheung Wan, exit B

Length 1.9km; one hour

🍴 Take a Break

Doppio Zero Trattoria (www.doppiozero.com.hk; basement, Pemberton, 22 Bonham Strand, Sheung Wan; 🕐lunch & dinner Mon-Sat, 11am-4pm Sun; Ⓜ Sheung Wan, exit A2)

Herbal medicines, Ko Shing St

IMAGEMORE CO. LTD/GETTY IMAGES ©

❶ Dried Seafood Shops

From the Sutherland St stop of the Kennedy Town tram, have a look at (and a sniff of) Des Voeux Rd West's many dried seafood shops, piled with all manner of desiccated sea life: scallops, abalone, sea cucumber, oysters, conch and fish maw.

❷ Herbal-Medicine Traders

Head south on Ko Shing St to browse the positively medieval-sounding goods on offer from the herbal-medicine traders. At the end of Ko Shing St, re-enter Des Voeux Rd West and walk northeast. Continue along Connaught Rd Central, where you'll pass the Edwardian building housing the Western Market.

❸ Ginseng & Bird's Nest Shops

At the corner of Morrison St, walk south to Wing Lok St and Bonham Strand, which are both lined with shops selling ginseng and edible bird's nests, the latter made from the salivary excretions of cave swifts, and consumed (as a sweet soup) for their proven ability to regenerate human cells.

❹ Tai Ping Shan Temples

Turn right onto Queen's Rd Central and pass by shops selling paper funeral offerings for the dead. Climb up Possession St, then take a right into Hollywood Rd, a left into Po Yan St and then a left into Tai

Ping Shan Street, where you'll spot three temples. Look to the right for Pak Sing Ancestral Hall and Kwun Yum Temple, and to the left for Tai Sui Temple.

❺ Antique Shops

Head up Upper Station St to the start of Hollywood Rd's **antique shops**. There's a vast choice of curios, replicas and a few rare, mostly Chinese, treasures.

❻ Man Mo Temple

Continuing east on Hollywood Rd brings you to **Man Mo Temple** (p28), one of the oldest temples in the territory and dedicated to the civil and martial gods Man Cheung and Kwan Yu. From here catch bus 26 or head north towards the harbour for Sheung Wan MTR station on Des Voeux Rd.

Best
Views

CRISTIAN BAITG/GETTY IMAGES ©

Best Eye-Level Views

Star Ferry There's no better way to view Hong Kong's famous harbour. (p24)

Trams Turn the city into a carousel of moving images. (p72)

Happy Valley Racecourse Between mountains and high-rises, the ponies gallop. (p64)

Best Vantage Points

Tsim Sha Tsui East Promenade Face to face with Hong Kong's most iconic view. (p96)

Hong Kong Monetary Authority Information Centre Sweeping 55th-floor vistas by the edge of the water. (p34)

Bank of China Tower Views stretch all the way to Kowloon from the 42nd floor. (p32)

Best Mountain-Top Views

Tian Tan Buddha See Lantau Island from 523m above the sea. (p137)

Tai Long Wan Trail Billowing hills and secluded coves. (p129)

Tung Ping Chau Cliffs with strange rocks hang over surf-beaten beaches. (p129)

Best Views from a Park

Victoria Peak Revisit the city from top down. (p43)

Hong Kong Park Unique juxtaposition of skyscrapers and mountains. (p66)

Ocean Park Cable cars command views of the South China Sea. (p89)

Best Views from a Bar

Sevva So close to the HSBC Building, it's downright dizzying. (p38)

Felix Bar Awesome views of Tsim Sha Tsui, especially from the men's bathroom. (p108)

InterContinental Lobby Lounge Same as Tsim Sha Tsui East Promenade but with air-con. (p106)

Aqua Spirit A dramatic take on the Island skyline, especially at night. (p106)

Best
Temples

Most Historically Important

Tsing Shan Monastery Believed to be the founding site of Buddhism in Hong Kong. (p132)

Kun Iam Temple An important treaty was signed at this Macau temple in 1844. (p148)

Man Mo Temple Once a court of arbitration for the Chinese. (p28)

Oldest Temples

A-Ma Temple Macau's oldest temple was originally established in 1488. (p148)

Kun Iam Temple Macau's second-oldest temple (c 1627). (p148)

Tsing Shan Monastery Said to have been built in the Jin dynasty (1115–1234). (p132)

Best Non-Taoist Temples

Tsing Shan Monastery A charmingly modest temple that is one of Hong Kong's three oldest. (p132)

Khalsa Diwan Sikh Temple The city's largest Sikh temple. (p69)

Chi Lin Nunnery Wonderful faux-Tang dynasty architecture (c 1998). (p125)

Best Urban Temples

Tin Hau Temple Right in Yau Ma Tei's community hub. (p117)

Man Mo Temple This famous structure sits in Sheung Wan. (p28)

Pak Tai Temple Magnificent temple in Wan Chai. (p72)

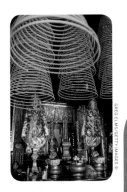

GREG ELMS/GETTY IMAGES ©

Quirkiest Temples

Hung Shing Temple Dark, mysterious, sits on a boulder. (p72)

Fook Tak Ancient Temple A tiny and smoky former shrine. (p100)

Temples with the Most Visual Impact

Sik Sik Yuen Wong Tai Sin Temple Colourful and flamboyant. (p125)

Man Mo Temple Incense coils hang from the ceiling. (p28)

Tian Tan Buddha The world's tallest seated outdoor bronze Buddha. (p137)

Best
Architecture

Over the centuries Hong Kong has played host to everything from Tao temples and Qing dynasty forts to Victorian churches and Edwardian hotels. But up until recently, the city's ceaseless cycle of deconstruction and reconstruction meant that the old and charming were often eagerly replaced by modern marvels.

Traditional Chinese

About the only examples of precolonial Chinese architecture left in urban Hong Kong are Tin Hau temples that date from the early to mid-19th century, including those at Tin Hau near Causeway Bay and Yau Ma Tei. For anything more substantial, you have to go to the New Territories, where walled villages, fortresses and ancient pagodas can be seen.

Colonial Architecture

Most of what is left of colonial architecture is on Hong Kong Island, especially in Central, though Tsim Sha Tsui on the Kowloon Peninsula also boasts quite a few examples. Some of Hong Kong's colonial architecture features adaptations for the tropical climate, just as some Chinese buildings have Western motifs.

Modern Architecture

Enthusiasts of modern architecture will have a field day here. Central and Wan Chai are especially rich showcases for modern and contemporary buildings – many designed by internationally celebrated architects.

IAN TROWER/GETTY IMAGES ©

☑ **Top Tips**

▸ For a list of historic structures, visit the website of the **Hong Kong Antiquities & Monuments Office** (☎2721 2326; www.amo.gov.hk; 136 Nathan Rd; ⏰9am-5pm Mon-Sat). Or visit in person: it's inside the Former Kowloon British School (p101) in Tsim Sha Tsui.

▸ For the latest on Hong Kong's preservation efforts, see www.heritage.gov.hk.

Kowloon–Canton Railway Clock Tower (p97)

Best Pre-Colonial Chinese Buildings

Man Mo Temple Built in the 1800s by wealthy Chinese merchants. (p28)

Ping Shan Heritage Trail The magnificent ancestral hall dates to the 1300s. (p133)

Best Colonial Structures

Central Police Station Compound Featuring late-Victorian and other styles. (p49)

Former Marine Police Headquarters One of the oldest (c 1884) and handsomest government buildings still around. (p100)

Clock Tower The only remaining structure of the old Kowloon–Canton Railway. (p25)

Best Fusion Architecture

Ruins of the Church of St Paul Sixteenth-century ruins in Macau. southern European with Asian details. (p142)

Mandarin's House A graceful Chinese residence in Macau, with hints of European influence. (p150)

Lui Seng Chun A Chinese 'shophouse' with Italian characteristics. (p118)

Best Contemporary Buildings

HSBC Building Masterpiece in late modern, high-tech style by Norman Foster. (p26)

Bank of China Tower A wonderful tower of cubes by IM Pei. (p32)

Asia Society Hong Kong Centre Sublime complex designed by Billie Tsien and Tod Williams. (p72)

Best
Museums & Galleries

Best Collections

Hong Kong Museum of Art Chinese art from Han to Qing dynasties, and Hong Kong art. (p97)

Liangyi Museum Eastern-inspired vanities and the world's best collection of classical Chinese furniture. (p32)

Macau Museum of Art Works by Macau's Chinese, Macanese and Western artists. (p148)

Best Buyable Art

Grotto Fine Art One of very few galleries with a focus on the best Hong Kong art. (p58)

AFA (Art for All Society) Excellent works by Macau's top artists. (p150)

Sin Sin Fine Art Edgy contemporary art from Europe and Asia. (p40)

Best 'People's' Art Spaces

Jockey Club Creative Arts Centre Artists' studios in a breezy former factory. (p125)

C&G Artpartment A socially-minded art space in the middle of Mong Kok. (p118)

Most Entertaining

Flagstaff House Museum of Tea Ware Featuring prized Chinese tea ware donated by a private collector. (p67)

Hong Kong Science Museum From gravity to tadpoles, all worldly phenomena explained. (p97)

Hong Kong Space Museum Try 'moonwalking' and eating astronaut ice cream. (p97)

GREG ELMS/GETTY IMAGES ©

☑ Top Tips

▶ **Hong Kong Art Walk** (www.hongkongartwalk.com) features over 60 galleries on Hong Kong Island opening their doors to visitors and entertaining with food and wine for one night in March.

▶ Art Basel Hong Kong (p81) in May sees hundreds of galleries and dealers from the world over participating to attract potential buyers and art collectors.

Best
Parks & Gardens

Best for Wildlife

Hong Kong Wetland Park Watch migratory birds in a natural setting. (p132)

Mai Po Marsh Nature Reserve For 380 species of birds. (p132)

Hong Kong Zoological & Botanical Gardens A collection of birds, beasts and plants. (p33)

Best for Human-Made Beauty

Victoria Peak Garden Restored 'Victorian' garden of a former governor's summer lodge. (p43)

Hong Kong Park Artificial waterfalls and ponds furnished with real waterfowl. (p66)

Most Secluded

Victoria Peak Garden Serene and romantic. (p43)

Mai Po Marsh Nature Reserve Birds are louder than people here, most of the time. (p132)

Middle Road Children's Playground There are very few people here on weekdays. (p101)

Best for a Picnic

Victoria Peak Garden Tea-party in style at this faux-Victorian garden with gazebos. (p43)

Victoria Park No shortage of plush blades where you can soak up the sun. (p74)

Kowloon Park Take your pick from lawn, bench or concrete at this former barracks. (p102)

Best for People-Watching

Middle Road Children's Playground Breezy park frequented by all ages and ethnicities. (p101)

BRIAN D CRUICKSHANK/GETTY IMAGES ©

☑ **Top Tip**

▶ For a longer list of Hong Kong's green green grass, visit http://lawnmap.org.

Kowloon Park Locals come to chat, picnic, swim, jog and practise kung fu. (p102)

Victoria Park Hang-out of Chinese families and, on Sundays, domestic helpers. (p74)

Ocean Park An awesome theme park packed with locals and tourists during holidays. (p89)

Best
Shopping

Everyone knows Hong Kong as a place of neon-lit retail pilgrimage. This city is positively stuffed with swanky shopping malls and brand-name boutiques. These are supplemented by the city's own retail trailblazers and creative local designers.

ANDREA COLANTONI/GETTY IMAGES ©

Clothing

The best place to find designer brands and luxury stores is in the malls. For something more unique, there are cool independent stores opened by local designers and retailers, especially in Sheung Wan, Wan Chai and Tsim Sha Tsui. You'll see some brilliant pieces, but the range is limited simply because these places are few and far between. The best hunting grounds for low-cost garments are the street markets.

Electronics

One of the cheapest places in the world for electronics and digitals, Hong Kong has a plethora of gadget shops. As a rule of thumb do not buy from street-level shops on Nathan Rd. Plenty of camera shops and computer malls are honest, though some shops in computer malls have been known to sell used items as new.

Antiques

Hong Kong has a rich array of Asian antiques on offer, especially Chinese, but expert reproductions abound. Serious buyers will restrict themselves to reputable antique shops and auction houses such as Christie's, especially at its auctions in spring and autumn when you'll find some excellent authentic pieces.

☑ **Top Tips**

▶ There's no sales tax in Hong Kong for most goods.

▶ Direct complaints to Hong Kong Tourism Board's **Quality Tourism Services** (QTS; ☎2806 2823; www. qtshk.com) or **Hong Kong Consumer Council** (☎2929 2222; www.consumer. org.hk; ⊙9am-5.45pm Mon-Fri).

KIMBERLEY COOLE/GETTY IMAGES ©

Shopping centre, Kowloon

Best for Fashion

Daydream Nation Edgy and romantic streetwear by Kay Wong. (p82)

Hulu 10 Modernised Chinese tunics, jackets and dresses. (p59)

Horizon Plaza Twenty-eight floors of fashion and furniture. (p92)

Best for Period Pieces

Arch Angel Antiques Tombware, urns and smaller pieces. (p59)

Lam Gallery Chinese antiques, especially sculptures. (p60)

Wattis Fine Art Ancient maps and old photos. (p59)

Best for Souvenirs

G.O.D. Hip, retro, design-oriented goods. (p92)

Shanghai Tang Clothes and homeware in modern chinoiserie style. (p39)

Best for Digital Gadgets

Wan Chai Computer Centre Almost everything computer-related. (p82)

Photo Scientific Professional photographers shop here. (p60)

Ap Liu Street Flea Market New and used digital and electronic appliances. (p125)

Most Specialised

Bruce Lee Club Shop and mini-museum devoted to the kung-fu icon. (p122)

Armoury Bespoke tailoring for the modern gentlemen. (p40)

Fook Ming Tong Tea Shop Good Chinese tea. (p40)

Best Speciality Malls

Rise Shopping Arcade Heaving with tiny fashion and accessory boutiques. (p111)

Sino Centre Manga, speciality magazines, used CDs. (p123)

Best
Markets

Best Speciality Markets

Cat Street Bazaar
Curios and (mostly) faux period pieces outdoors and in shops. (p35)

Jade Market Jade pendants, bracelets and other accessories in a covered setting. (p117)

Ap Liu Street Flea Market Electronic and digital gadgets, used and new; in stalls and outdoors. (p125)

Best for Clothing

Stanley Market T-shirts, children's wear, Chinese-style garb in a maze of shops. (p87)

Tung Choi Street Market Cheap casual clothing in stalls lining a street. (p123)

Li Yuen Street East & West Hawkers selling clothes, shoes and handbags crammed into alleyways. (p40)

Best for Atmosphere

Temple Street Night Market A sensory journey under the moon. (p114)

Wholesale Fruit Market These historic buildings in Yau Ma Tei come alive in the wee hours. (p118)

Wan Chai's Markets The shops and stalls here are positively buzzing with local life. (p83)

Most Eclectic Markets

Temple Street Night Market Fortune tellers, Cantonese opera performers, hawkers, hookers and street food. (p114)

Ap Liu Street Flea Market Quirky finds like rare batteries and satellite dishes. (p125)

Stanley Market Clothes, Chinese souvenirs, lacework, even wetsuits; and food nearby. (p87)

PETE SEAWARD/LONELY PLANET ©

Wan Chai's Markets
Food, funerary offerings, incense and spice shops along several streets. (p83)

Best for Fresh Food

Wan Chai's Markets
Live produce, fresh noodles and all manner of spices along the street. (p83)

Ap Lei Chau Market Cooked Food Centre
Huge selection of live fish and crustaceans inside a building. (p90)

Wholesale Fruit Market Retail is sometimes possible at this moody century-old market in Yau Ma Tei. (p118)

Best
Activities

MARK HANNAFORD/GETTY IMAGES ©

Most Scenic Hiking Trails

High Island Reservoir East Dam Trail Natural and human-made sublimity. (p128)

Tai Long Wan Trail A popular route with views of secluded beaches. (p129)

Shing Mun Reservoir Trail A serene reservoir surrounded by paperbark trees. (p129)

Best Beaches

South Bay A gem of a beach, especially at night. (p87)

Middle Bay A quaint beach popular with scenesters. (p87)

St Stephen's Beach Close to Stanley but without the crowds. (p87)

Best for Meeting People

Salsa, tango or swing Party with locals and expats at club nights. (p58)

Taichi Other travellers will likely be taking the same class. (p100)

Southorn Playground At any time of the day you'll meet locals from different walks of life. (p68)

Best for Pampering

Happy Foot Reflexology Centre Foot and body massage. (p50)

Ten Feet Tall Feet kneading in a design-oriented parlour. (p39)

Flawless Hong Kong Feel-good massages and beauty treatments for glamour-conscious hipsters. (p50)

☑ **Top Tips**

▶ **Hong Kong Ultimate Frisbee Association** (www.hkupa.com) has twice-a-week pickups, and a major Hat Tournament (accompanied by much partying) in May.

▶ **Casual Football Network** (http://casualfootball.net) has at least three games of football (soccer) a week.

▶ **Natural Excursion Ideals** (☎9300 5197; www.kayak-and-hike.com) runs hiking and kayaking trips.

Best
Fine Dining

MALCOLM AINSWORTH/GETTY IMAGES ©

Those with a large pocket are spoilt for choice in Hong Kong when it comes to haute cuisine, from braised abalone and lobster sashimi to the fancy molecular creations of the latest celebrity chef. Prices at the top addresses can be steep, but the city's gourmands don't seem to mind – the restaurants are fully booked almost any night of the week.

Haute Cantonese

Hong Kong's dominant cuisine is Cantonese, the most sophisticated of China's eight regional cuisines. It's one that's known for complex cooking methods, an obsession with freshness, and its wide range of ingredients. The coastal location has also meant that Cantonese kitchens enjoy access to some very costly marine life, such as deep-sea fish and gigantic lobsters. That is why even northern Chinese cooks would acknowledge the superiority of their Cantonese colleagues in making the best of exclusive items like abalone.

Celebrity Chefs

Hong Kong's affluent and cosmopolitan population loves foreign food, especially Japanese and European. This is evidenced by the sheer number of exclusive sushi bars you can find in town and the number of eponymous restaurants opened by international celebrity chefs such as Nobuyuki 'Nobu' Matsuhisa, Joël Robuchon and Pierre Gagnaire.

☑ **Top Tips**

▶ A few of our favourite English-language food blogs for getting the up-to-date dirt on restaurants new and old:

That Food Cray (www.thatfoodcray.com)

Sassy Hong Kong (www.sassyhong-kong.com)

e-Ting (www.e-ting-food.com)

Food Craver (www.foodcraver.hk)

Hungry Hong Kong (http://hungryhk.blogspot.hk)

HIPPO STUDIO/GETTY IMAGES ©

Steamed abalone

Best Overall

Gaddi's Impeccable French food and pristine service. (p103)

Sushi Kuu Fresh seafood in generous portions. (p51)

Yin Yang Chinese dishes full of pleasant surprises. (p76)

Best for Chinese

Yin Yang Chinese with modern influences. (p76)

Chairman Cantonese cooked with top-notch ingredients. (p36)

Boss Worthy competitor of the Chairman above. (p35)

Best for Seafood

Chuen Kee Seafood Restaurant Harbourfront setting featuring tanks brimming with marine life. (p133)

Ap Lei Chau Market Cooked Food Centre Great seafood at noisy indoor hawker centre. (p90)

Best for European

Gaddi's French food masterfully prepared since 1953. (p103)

Ammo Spanish tapas and Italian mains. (p73)

Best for Ambience

Ammo Chic ammunition-inspired decor in the hills of Admiralty. (p73)

Yin Yang Faux-rustic decor inside a historic building. (p76)

Yè Shanghai Elegant interiors with huge windows. (p104)

Best for Views

Lung King Heen Sweeping harbour views. (p35)

Caprice Harbour sights run the length of the room through a wall of glass. (p38)

Best for Japanese

Sushi Kuu One of the best sushi bars in town. (p51)

Iroha Japanese-style grilled meat specialist with a huge range of cuts. (p69)

Irori Innovative sushi and cooked dishes with a modern twist. (p77)

Best
Budget Eats & Street Food

It is not difficult to eat well and cheaply in Hong Kong, compared to Tokyo or London. If you're looking to spend under HK$200 per person on a meal, there are good Chinese and South Asian options aplenty. For anything under HK$100, your dining room would be a noodle and congee shop, *cha chaan tang*, *dai pai dong* or fast-food chain.

Cha Chaan Tang

The quintessential Hong Kong eatery, the 'tea cafe' appeared in the 1940s to provide cheap Western-style snacks to people who couldn't afford Earl Grey and cucumber sandwiches. Most, like Mido Café (p120) serve sandwiches, noodles, and tea or coffee with milk; some also serve rice dishes, curries and seafood, and Western-style pastries such as egg custard tarts.

Dai Pai Dong

After WWII the government issued licences to the families of deceased civil servants so that they could operate food stalls for a living. The licence was physically big, so locals referred to these eateries as 'big licence stall' *(dai pai dong)*. Traditionally, they are open-air hawker-style places, but many have been relocated to 'cooked-food centres' in buildings for easier management. Operators may serve anything from congee and sandwiches to hotpots and seafood.

THOMAS RUECKER/GETTY IMAGES ©

☑ **Top Tips**

▶ To save money, go to a *cha chaan tang* (tea house) for the breakfast set or tea set. Portions are slightly smaller than a la carte. All sets come with a drink.

Best Dai Pai Dong

Temple Street Night Market Hawkers, vendors, Cantonese opera singers, and fortune-tellers. (p114)

Ap Lei Chau Market Cooked Food Centre It'll also cook seafood bought from the market downstairs. (p90)

Yue Hing Hong Kong–style milk tea and unusual sandwiches, consumed al fresco. (p51)

Temple Street Night Market (p114)

Best Noodle & Congee Shops

Sun Sin Excellent noodles in curry or tomato soup. (p119)

Good Hope Noodle Humble Michelin-crowned noodle and congee place. (p120)

Tasty Congee & Noodle Wonton Shop Simple, well-executed food in upmarket surrounds. (p36)

Best Chinese Budget Eateries

Din Tai Fung Shanghainese and northern classics by a Taiwanese chain. (p104)

Ser Wong Fun Old-school Cantonese dishes and snake soup. (p51)

Spring Deer Solid northern Chinese fare; very busy. (p104)

Best Asian Eateries

Old Bazaar Kitchen Excellent Malaysian and Chinese-Malaysian dishes. (p76)

Sushi Kuu Fresh Japanese seafood painstakingly prepared, beautifully presented. (p51)

Woodlands A great choice for South Indian vegetarian fare. (p103)

Best European Eateries

La Creperie The most legitimate crepes and galettes in town. (p160)

Life Cafe Creative veggie or vegan fare for dine-in or takeaway. (p52)

Best for Local Edibles

Honeymoon Dessert Overwhelming selection of Chinese and Western desserts. (p134)

Yiu Fung Store Preserved plums, candied melon, dried orange peel and more. (p83)

Kowloon Soy Company An old shop famous for its Chinese condiments and snacks. (p61)

Best
Dim Sum

Dim sum are tidbits consumed with tea for breakfast or lunch. The term literally means 'to touch the heart' and the act of eating dim sum – a strictly Cantonese practice – is yum cha, meaning 'to drink tea'. Each dish, often containing two to four morsels steamed in a bamboo basket, is meant to be shared.

XPACIFICA/GETTY IMAGES ©

Best Overall

Luk Yu Tea House Old-school excellence; unbeatable decor. (p51)

Tim Ho Wan, the Dim Sum Specialists Cheap and cheery; comes with Michelin stars. (p38)

Boss Flavourful yet healthy dim sum in a modern setting. (p35)

Best Budget Places

Tai Wing Wah Traditional selections in far-flung Yuen Long. (p134)

Tim Ho Wan, the Dim Sum Specialists Possibly the world's cheapest Michelin-lauded dim sum. (p38)

Best Midrange Dim Sum

Luk Yu Tea House Hong Kong's most famous teahouse. (p51)

City Hall Maxim's Palace Massive selection in a massive dining room. (p38)

Yè Shanghai Popular Cantonese selections plus delectable Shanghainese tidbits. (p104)

Best Luxury Tidbits

Lung King Heen Top-notch vistas and Michelin-crowned creations. (p35)

Boss Exquisite food, immaculate service. (p35)

Best for Ambience

Luk Yu Tea House Eastern art-deco setting with whirling fans and stained-glass windows. (p51)

Lung King Heen A sleek and modern dining room with awesome views. (p35)

Jumbo Kingdom Floating Restaurant Memorable kitsch and harbour views, almost like a movie set. (p91)

City Hall Maxim's Palace A typical yum cha experience in a large noisy hall. (p38)

Best **Culture**

Hong Kong's hybrid culture is complex and fascinating, due to its different trajectory of development from the rest of China. Colonisation has Westernised the city, yet the influences of traditional Lingnan culture, dominant in Guǎngdōng and other areas of southern China, are also apparent.

GREG ELMS/GETTY IMAGES ©

Best for Food Culture

Mido Café Homegrown Chinese and pseudo-Western food in a retro setting. (p120)

Luk Yu Tea House Dim sum as delicious as the Chinese art-deco interiors. (p51)

Yin Yang Classic Hong Kong food with an elegant and healthy twist. (p76)

Best for Local Culture

Hong Kong Museum of History All about Hong Kong: birth, teething, growing pains and all. (p99)

Ap Liu Street Flea Market Browse with comb-over uncles at this street-level gadget heaven. (p125)

Wholesale Fruit Market A century-old fruit market that's alive and kicking, under the moon. (p118)

Sino Centre A speciality mall for anime, discontinued magazines, figurines and other geeky collectibles. (p123)

G.O.D. Cheeky Hong Kong–inspired lifestyle items. (p92)

Sing-Along Parlours Interestingly shabby places of entertainment unique to Yau Ma Tei. (p118)

Best for Indigenous Culture

Ping Shan Heritage Trail Walled villages of one of Hong Kong's earliest clans. (p133)

Heritage Museum See the customs and rituals of the Tanka, Hakka and Puntay people. (p132)

Best for Religious Culture

Tsing Shan Monastery The city's oldest Buddhist temple was supposedly founded by Pui To, an Indian monk travelling in a wooden cup. (p132)

St John's Cathedral East Asia's oldest Anglican church offered its first Sunday service in 1849. (p32)

Kowloon Mosque & Islamic Centre Hong Kong's largest mosque has over 70,000 Muslims under its dome. (p102)

Man Mo Temple An important social and spiritual (Taoist) hub for the Chinese community in colonial days. (p28)

Khalsa Diwan Sikh Temple Founded by Sikh members of the British in the 1900s. (p69)

Best
Drinking & Nightlife

Lan Kwai Fong and Soho are the best areas for bars; they're full of life and revellers almost every night. Pubs in Wan Chai are cheaper and more relaxed, though a few sleek addresses have sprung up in the Star St neighbourhood. Watering holes in Tsim Sha Tsui tend to attract a more local clientele.

Happy Hour

During certain hours of the day, most pubs, bars and a few clubs give discounts on drinks (usually from a third to half off) or offer two-for-one deals. Happy hour is usually in the late afternoon or early evening – 4pm to 8pm, say – but times vary widely from place to place. Depending on the season, the day of the week and the location, some happy hours run from noon until 10pm, and some start up again after midnight.

Dress Code

Usually smart casual is good enough for most clubs, but patrons wearing shorts and flip-flops will not be admitted. Jeans are popular in Hong Kong and these are sometimes worn with heels or a blazer for a more put-together look. Hong Kong's clubbers can be style-conscious, so dress to impress!

How Much?

It's not cheap to drink in Hong Kong. An all-night boozy tour of the city's drinking landscape will set you back at least HK$800. That said, it's possible to cut corners while still soaking up the atmosphere. Buy your drinks from a convenience store and hang out with the paying revellers outside the bars – lots of youngsters do that!

☑ **Top Tips**

▶ Bars open at noon or 6pm and stay open until 2am to 6am; Wan Chai bars stay open the latest. Cafes usually open between 8am and 11am and close between 5pm and 11pm.

▶ For the latest information, check out **Time Out** (www.timeout.com.hk) and **HK Magazine** (http://hk.asia-city.com)

Club 71 (p47)

Most Stylish Decor

Sevva Sleek and tastefully dramatic. (p38)

Pawn Former pawn shop repackaged with modern trappings, and offering a colourful list of cocktails. (p79)

Felix Bar Designed by Philippe Starck. (p108)

Best for Meeting Nonposeurs

Club 71 Artist and activist hang-out. (p47)

Liberty Exchange Haunt of finance-industry types. (p39)

Senses 99 Party in someone's home. (p58)

Best for Live Music

Peel Fresco Excellent jazz. (p57)

Grappa's Cellar Swing, electronic, jazz. (p39)

Fringe Club Indie gigs in the intimate spaces of a former dairy. (p57)

Best Pubs

Globe Spacious and homey. (p54)

Delaney's A lively, two-floor Irish pub. (p79)

Ned Kelly's Last Stand Quirky and loads of fun, with a live band. (p108)

Best Whisky Bars

Macallan Whisky Bar & Lounge This Macau whisky bar is arguably the best in either city. (p153)

Angel's Share Whisky Bar Clubby place specialising in Irish whisky. (p53)

Executive Bar Japanese-style bar; by appointment only. (p78)

Butler Japanese bartending excellence in Kowloon. (p106)

Best Wine Spots

Crown Wine Cellars Great bottles in a historic building. (p90)

Central Wine Club Over 500 bottles await at this fancy, upmarket place. (p54)

Best
Gay & Lesbian

While Hong Kong's gay scene may not have the vibrancy or visibility of cities like Sydney, it has made huge strides in recent years. Two decades ago, it had no more than a couple of grotty speakeasies. Today Hong Kong counts more than two-dozen bars and clubs, and just as many gay-oriented saunas.

Attitude to Homosexuality

It was only in 1991 that the Crimes (Amendment) Ordinance removed criminal penalties for homosexual acts between consenting adults over the age of 18 (the criminal laws against male homosexuality were initially a product of British colonialism, with a maximum sentence of life imprisonment). Since then, gay groups have been lobbying for legislation to address the issue of discrimination on the grounds of sexual orientation, but to date there's still no law against it in Hong Kong. Neither is there legal recognition for same-sex marriages. That said, Hong Kong Chinese society is, in general, a lot more accepting of homosexuality than it was 10 years ago.

GLOW IMAGES, INC/GETTY IMAGES ©

☑ Top Tips

▶ For information on Hong Kong Pride Parade visit http:// hkpride.net.

▶ Les Peches (p53) has monthly events for lesbians and bisexual women.

▶ **Dim Sum** (http:// dimsum-hk.com) has free monthly listings.

Best Bars & Clubs

T:ME A small and trendy bar off Hollywood Rd. (p54)

Volume Cocktail bar with a dance floor. (p54)

Best for Shopping

D-mop Edgy street fashion. (p83)

G.O.D. Lifestyle products with cheeky retro motifs. (p92)

Horizon Plaza Furniture and clothing. (p92)

Armoury For all things dapper, tailored and off-the-rack. (p40)

Joyce Eclectic (and expensive) collection of international and local brands. (p41)

Best
Escapes

. . . .

Hong Kong may seem like the ultimate metropolis, but contrast is never more than an hour away. Close to three-quarters of the territory is countryside – rolling hills, country and marine parks full of breathtaking vistas – which offers plenty of opportunities for a much needed escape.

. . . .

DAVID EVANS/GETTY IMAGES ©

Best Hiking Escapes

Bride's Pool – Lai Chi Wo Hakka village with a well-preserved 'feng shui' forest. (p129)

Ma On Shan Country Park Trail Passes an old iron miners' village and meadows full of butterflies. (p129)

Tung Ping Chau Walking Trail Volcanic rock formations from aeons ago. (p129)

Shing Mun Reservoir Trail Vintage reservoir structures and paperbark trees. (p129)

High Island Reservoir East Dam Trail Natural and manufactured sublimity. (p128)

Best Beach Escapes

Tai Long Wan Trail Beaches Secluded, white-sanded beaches along a hiking trail. (p129)

St Stephen's Beach A small and off-the-way beach in Stanley. (p87)

Best Island Escapes

Lamma Hong Kong's most relaxing outlying island. (p138)

Lantau Serenity prevails in most corners of Hong Kong's largest island.

Best Urban Escapes

Peak Garden A faux-Victorian garden on Victoria Peak. (p43)

☑ **Top Tips**

▶ Hong Kong's efficient MTR system and comprehensive bus network means you can take to the hills or the beaches within an hour from the nearest urban centre.

▶ If hiking in the summer, bring swimming gear for an impromptu dip.

Middle Road Children's Playground Quiet on weekdays; on weekends, children's laughter is your background music. (p101)

Best
For Kids

Hong Kong is a great travel destination for kids, though the crowds, traffic and pollution might take some parents a little getting used to. Food and sanitation are of a high standard. The city is jam-packed with things to entertain the young ones, often just a hop, skip and jump away from attractions for you.

ABASSOULTUM/GETTY IMAGES ©

Dolphin Watching

See the second-smartest animal on earth in the wild – and it's in bubble-gum pink! **Hong Kong Dolphinwatch** (香港海豚觀察; ☎2984 1414; www. hkdolphinwatch.com; 15th fl, Middle Block, 1528A Star House, 3 Salisbury Rd, Tsim Sha Tsui; adult/child HK$420/210; ⊙cruises Wed, Fri & Sun) runs three four-hour tours a week to waters where Chinese White Dolphins may be sighted.

Best for Young Children

Hong Kong Space Museum Plenty of opportunities for kids to test their motor skills. (p97)

Hong Kong Science Museum Three storeys of action-packed displays, including a play area for toddlers. (p97)

Middle Road Children's Playground Swings, slides and climbing facilities. (p101)

Hong Kong Zoological & Botanical Gardens Flamingos, baboons, storks and tortoises. (p33)

Best for Older Kids & Preteens

Ocean Park Hong Kong's premier amusement park. (p89)

Hong Kong Science Museum Multimedia, hands-on displays spread out over three storeys. (p97)

☑ **Top Tips**

▶ For more ideas check out this booklet from the tourism board: www.discoverhongkong.com/ promotions/family/ eng/html/front/index.html.

▶ Nursing rooms are available in large malls and museums.

▶ **Rent-a-Mum** (☎2523 4868; www. rent-a-mum.com; per hr from HK$180) and **In Safe Hands** (☎9820 3363, 2323 2676; www. insafehands.com.hk; per hr from HK$200, plus transport costs) have child-minding services (note transport charges may be added).

Hong Kong Park (p66)

Hong Kong Wetland Park Themed exhibits, a theatre and play facilities. (p132)

Hong Kong Heritage Museum The museum has a slightly chaotic but fun (for kids) children's discovery centre. (p132)

Hong Kong Maritime Museum Plenty to fire junior's imagination – pirate mannequins, real treasures etc – at this excellent place. (p34)

Best Shopping for Kids

Tai Yuen Street in Wan Chai Known for its traditional toy shops. (p83)

Ocean Terminal The ground floor has a collection of shops for kids. (p111)

Horizon Plaza Has megastores selling kids' books and clothing. (p92)

Best Transport for Kids

Peak Tram A gravity-defying vehicle that takes you to the age-defying mannequins at Madame Tussauds. (p42)

Star Ferry Your mini-mariner will have a blast naming passing vessels on Victoria Harbour. (p24)

Trams A vehicle that rattles, clanks and sways amid heavy traffic can be exhilarating. (p72)

MTR Interestingly colour-coded; it's fun to guess the meaning behind the choice of colour.

Best Dining for Kids

Jumbo Kingdom Floating Restaurant A popular movie set decked out in dragon-and-phoenix carvings. (p91)

Tree Cafe Ham-and-cheese sandwiches, hot chocolate and toys. (p92)

Honeymoon Dessert Asian and Western desserts. (p134)

Dumpling Yuan Nine delicious varieties of dumplings will keep junior fed and your wallet happy. (p53)

Vbest Tea House Healthy and tasty Cantonese comfort food. (p52)

Yue Hing Imagine a spam and egg sandwich with peanut butter! (p51)

Best
For Free

Hong Kong is not a cheap city to visit by any means, but sometimes a little imagination can help keep your pockets full. Not only that, going creatively cheap can sometimes reward you with riches the moneyed never even dream about. Here are some free (or almost free) options in addition to parks, beaches, temples and markets.

LONELY PLANET/GETTY IMAGES ©

Best History for Free

Ping Shan Heritage Trail Magnificent buildings in a walled village. (p133)

Former Marine Police Headquarters One of the oldest remaining government buildings. (p100)

Hong Kong Cemetery Reads like a 'who's who' of dead Hong Kong. (p69)

Best Culture for Free

Street Music Concerts Excellent concerts under the stars. (p80)

Taichi A cheap taichi lesson by the Tsim Sha Tsui harbourfront. (p100)

PMQ A new art hub in former police quarters. (p49)

Best Vibe for Free

Happy Valley Racecourse Bring wine and chestnuts; win more than HK$10 and you'll cover your admission. (p64)

Chungking Mansions A global village in the heart of Tsim Sha Tsui. (p100)

Southorn Playground The social hub of old Wan Chai. (p68)

☑ **Top Tip**

▶ For a cheaper trip to the movies, visit on Tuesdays, when you can pay up to HK$25 less.

Best Art for Free

C&G Artpartment Politically minded art in Mong Kok. (p118)

Jockey Club Creative Arts Centre Artists' studios in a former factory. (p125)

Survival Guide

Survival Guide

Before You Go

When to Go

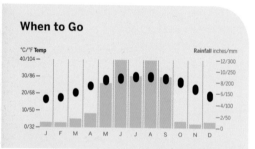

°C/°F **Temp**
40/104 —
30/86 —
20/68 —
10/50 —
0/32 —

Rainfall inches/mm
—12/300
—10/250
—8/200
—6/150
—4/100
—2/50
—0

J F M A M J J A S O N D

➡ **Spring (Mar-May)**
Asia's top film festival, a rugby tournament, an art fair and deities' birthdays await in the warm and wet city.

➡ **Summer (Jun-Aug)**
Something hot (the beach, a new wardrobe), something wet (dragon-boat races, beer): your antidotes to sultry summers.

➡ **Autumn (Sep-Nov)**
Head for the hills by day, enjoy an arts festival by night – autumn is the best time to visit Hong Kong.

➡ **Winter (Dec-Feb)**
Chilly with occasional rain, Hong Kong celebrates Chinese New Year under Christmas lights.

Book Your Stay

☑ **Top Tip** Visiting outside peak periods can save you up to 50% off rack rates if you book online.

➡ If you're on a tight budget, your options on Hong Kong Island are more or less limited to busy Causeway Bay, which is great for shopping. Over the water, Tsim Sha Tsui is crammed with budget places, mostly tiny guesthouses, including a few new ones with a good vibe.

➡ For those seeking a midpriced stay, Wan Chai, on Hong Kong Island, has plenty of midrange places, some at reasonable rates. Tsim Sha Tsui and Kowloon, however, offer by far the most bang for your midrange buck.

➡ Accommodation high seasons are from March to April, October to November, and around Chinese New Year (late January or February).

Dos & Don'ts

Clothing Beyond the suited realm of business, smart-casual dress is acceptable even at swish restaurants.

Colours Some colours hold different symbolic meaning in Chinese culture compared to Western cultures. Red means happiness and good luck (though writing in red can convey anger). White symbolises death, so avoid giving white flowers (except at funerals).

Dining In Hong Kong dining is an all-in affair: everyone shares dishes and chats loudly. If you can't manage chopsticks, don't be afraid to ask for a fork (most Chinese restaurants have them). Don't stick chopsticks upright into a bowl of rice as they can look like incense sticks in a bowl of ashes (an offering to the dead). When someone pours you tea, tap the table lightly with your index and middle finger.

Gifts If you want to give flowers, chocolates or wine to someone, they may appear reluctant to accept for fear of seeming greedy, but insist and they'll give in and take them.

Visa Most nationalities can stay in Hong Kong for up to 90 days. Check visa requirements on www.immd.gov.hk.

Useful Websites

Lonely Planet (www.lonelyplanet.com) Author-recommended reviews and online booking.

Hong Kong Youth Hostels Association (www.yha.org.hk) Hostelling International (HI)–affiliated hostels.

Country & Marine Parks Authority (www.afcd.gov.hk) Maintains 41 campsites.

Hong Kong Tourism Board (www.discoverhongkong.com) Lets you search some 200 licensed hotels and guesthouses in Hong Kong.

Hong Kong Hotels Association (www.hkha.org) For the booking of hotels under the association.

Best Budget

Salisbury (www.ymcahk.org.hk) Ticks the boxes for views, facilities, service, and location (Tsim Sha Tsui), but difficult to book and conditions apply.

Urban Pack (www.urbanpack.com) Great-value dorm rooms and friendly owners who'll take you partying, in the heart of Tsim Sha Tsui.

YHA Mei Ho House Youth Hostel (www.meihohouse.hk) Clean, airy rooms inside a heritage building with its own museum; it's located in Shek Kip Mei.

YesInn (www.yesinn.com) A lively hostel in Wan Chai with a great backpacker vibe.

Best Midrange

Hotel LKF (www.hotel-lkf.com.hk) Quiet, well-equipped rooms in the thick of the Lan Kwai Fong action.

Madera Hong Kong (www.hotelmadera.com.hk) Welcoming rooms and tasteful decor make up this boutique hotel in Yau Ma Tei.

Mira Moon (www.miramoonhotel.com) Warm service, ecofriendly design, and decor inspired by Chinese folklore in Wan Chai.

Fleming (www.thefleming.com) A compact boutique hotel with all the necessary trimmings in a quiet corner of Wan Chai.

Best Top End

Mandarin Oriental (www.mandarinoriental.com/hongkong/) The award-winning Mandarin offers understated elegance and exemplary service in the heart of Central.

Upper House (www.upperhouse.com) Ecofriendly, zen-inspired luxury in Admiralty.

Hotel Icon (www.hotel-icon.com) Excellent value teaching hotel in a less-visited part of Tsim Sha Tsui.

Hyatt Regency Tsim Sha Tsui (http://hongkong.tsimshatsui.hyatt.com) Plush rooms and warm service in a quiet corner of Tsim Sha Tsui.

Best for Families

InterContinental Hong Kong (www.intercontinental.com) Nearby museums and a playground, free stay for children under 12, and kid-friendly restaurants make this a great option in Tsim Sha Tsui.

Salisbury (www.ymcahk.org.hk) Offers nice family rooms, proximity to playground and museums, and an impressive array of sports facilities in Tsim Sha Tsui.

BP International Hotel (www.bpih.com.hk) Family rooms with solid bunk beds right next to sprawling Kowloon Park in Tsim Sha Tsui.

Boat Moksha (www.airbnb.com/rooms/65117) A welcoming B&B on a houseboat moored in Aberdeen.

Arriving in Hong Kong

☑ **Top Tip** For the best way to get to your accommodation, see p17.

Hong Kong International Airport

➡ Hong Kong International Airport Express MTR train to city centre from 6am to 1.15am, HK$90 to HK$100.

➡ Major hotel and guesthouse areas on Hong Kong Island are served by Air Buses (every 10 to 30 minutes from 6am to midnight). For Central, Sheung Wan, Admiralty, Wan Chai and Causeway Bay take Air Bus A11 (HK$40); for the south take the A10 (HK$48); for Tsim Sha Tsui, Yau Ma Tei and Mong Kok take the A21 (HK$33). Buy your ticket at the booth near the airport bus stand.

➡ Taxi to city centre HK$220 to HK$360

Lo Wu or Lok Ma Chau

➡ If you cross the border from Shēnzhèn via the Lo Wu or Lok Ma Chau border gates, take the MTR East Rail line after passing through customs. Lo Wu and Lok Ma Chau MTR train to city centre from 5.55am to 1.30am (Lo Wu), from 6.38am to 10.55pm (Lok Ma Chau), both HK$48.

→ If you take cross-border buses from Guǎngdōng to Hong Kong, you'll need to alight from and reboard the buses before and after going through customs in Lo Wu or Lok Ma Chau. Almost all buses stop near MTR stations, so you can either change to MTR or taxi.

Macau Ferry Terminal

→ You can reach Hong Kong from Macau and Guǎngdōng by frequent ferry services. Macau to Hong Kong: Turbojet and Cotai Jet. Guǎngdōng to Hong Kong: Chu Kong Passenger Transportation Company.

→ You will arrive in Hong Kong at either the Hong Kong–Macau Ferry Terminal or the China Ferry Terminal. The former is located next to the Sheung Wan MTR station, which is stops

away from destinations on Hong Kong Island. The China Ferry Terminal is a 15-minute walk from Tsim Sha Tsui MTR station.

Getting Around

Bus
☑ **Best for...** rural destinations without any MTR stations nearby.

→ Hong Kong's extensive bus system runs from 5.30am or 6am up to 12.30am. **KMB** (www.kmb. hk) serves Kowloon and New Territories; **City**

Bus and **First Bus** (www. nwstbus.com.hk) serve Hong Kong Island. You will need exact change or an Octopus card.

Ferry
☑ **Best for...** crossing Victoria Harbour from Central to Tsim Sha Tsui or vice versa.

→ The ferry connects Hong Kong Island and Kowloon Peninsula via Victoria Harbour; it runs from 6.30am-11.30pm; fares are HK$2.50 to HK$3.40. Modern ferry fleets run between Central and the outlying islands.

Metro
☑ **Best for...** most urban destinations.

Tickets & Passes
The **Octopus card** (✆ 2266 2222; www.octopuscards.com) is a rechargeable 'smart card' that can be used on most forms of public transport, and allows you to make purchases at convenience stores and supermarkets.

For shorter stays there's the new MTR Tourist Day Pass (adult/child HK$55/25), valid on the MTR for 24 hours after the first use. Both can be bought at MTR stations.

Airport Express Travel Pass allows three days of unlimited travel on the MTR and one or two trips on the Airport Express (one/two trips $220/300).

→ The **Mass Transit Railway** (MTR; ☎2881 8888; www.mtr.com.hk; fares HK$4-25) has nine lines serving Hong Kong Island, Kowloon, and the New Territories.

Taxi

☑ **Best for...** late hours when the MTR has stopped running and traffic is light.

→ Hong Kong taxis are a bargain compared to taxis in other world-class cities. Some sample fares:

ROUTE	FARE
Central MTR station to Causeway Bay	HK$70
Central MTR station to Victoria Peak	HK$100
Central MTR station to Tsim Sha Tsui	HK$120
Tsim Sha Tsui to Sai Kung	HK$170
Tung Chung to Tian Tan Buddha	HK$150

Tram

☑ **Best for...** sightseeing and when you're not in a hurry.

→ For a flat fare of HK$2.50 (dropped in a box beside the driver as you disembark) you can rattle along the northern

coast of Hong Kong Island on a double-decker tram (6am-12.30am) for as far as you like, over 16km of track.

Essential Information

Business Hours

☑ **Top Tip** Banks and post offices are closed on Sundays.

→ Reviews in this book won't list business hours unless they differ from standard hours listed below.

Banks 9am–4.30pm Monday–Friday; some branches are also open 9am–12.30pm Saturday

Bars Noon or 6pm to 2am–6am

Post offices 9.30am–5pm Monday–Friday, 9.30am–1pm Saturday

Restaurants Smaller eateries from 7am or 8am to 11pm; formal restaurants from 11am to at least 10pm

Shops 10am or 11am to 9pm or 10pm

Customs Regulations

→ The duty-free allowance for visitors arriving in Hong Kong (including those coming from Macau and mainland China) is 19 cigarettes (or one cigar or 25g of tobacco) and 1L of spirits. There are few other import taxes.

Electricity

220V/50Hz

Emergency

Fire, Police & Ambulance (☎999)

Internet Access

➜ Wi-fi is widely available. CSL sells Discover Hong Kong Tourist SIM Card (HK$69), which provides 3G connection and unlimited wi-fi access to close to 10,000 hotspots.

➜ Free wi-fi can be found at parks, public libraries, museums, cafes, and Hong Kong International Airport. For locations, see www.gov.hk/en/theme/wifi/location.

Money

Local Currency

➜ Hong Kong uses Hong Kong currency but some shops and restaurants also accept rénmínbì.

➜ Macau uses pataca and most places accept Hong Kong currency as well.

➜ ATMs are widely available; international travellers can withdraw funds from home accounts. Many allow cash withdrawal with foreign cards, usually with a transaction surcharge.

Credit Cards

Visa, MasterCard, American Express, Diners Club and JCB are widely accepted.

Tipping

➜ Hong Kong is not a particularly tip-conscious place; taxi drivers only expect you to round up to the nearest dollar.

➜ Tip hotel porters HK$10 to HK$20.

➜ Most hotels and many restaurants add a 10% service charge to the bill.

Organised Tours

Hong Kong Tourism Board (p194) runs some of the best tours; tours run by individual companies can usually be booked at any HKTB branch.

Star Ferry Harbour Tour (☎2118 6201; www.starferry.com.hk/tour) is the easiest way to see the full extent of Victoria Harbour from sea level; most depart from the Star Ferry Pier in Tsim Sha Tsui.

Little Adventures in Hong Kong (www.littleadventuresinhongkong.com) Everything from food crawls to history walks.

Money-Saving Tips

➜ Take the super-efficient MTR and only change to taxi if needed.

➜ Head to museums on Wednesdays when they have free entry, and visit night markets (also free).

Public Holidays

New Year's Day 1 January

Chinese New Year 19–21 February 2015, 8–10 February 2016

Easter 3–7 April 2015, 25–28 March 2016

Ching Ming 5 April 2015, 3 April 2016

Labour Day 1 May

Buddha's Birthday 25 May 2015, 14 May 2016

Dragon Boat (Tuen Ng) Festival 20 June 2015, 9 June 2016

Hong Kong SAR Establishment Day 1 July

Mid-Autumn Festival 27 September 2015, 15 September 2016

China National Day
1 October

Chung Yeung 21 October 2015, 10 October 2016

Christmas Day
25 December

Boxing Day
26 December

Telephone

➡ Any GSM-compatible phone can be used in Hong Kong.

➡ CSL has retail outlets throughout the territory, where you can buy phonecards, mobile phones and accessories. A SIM card with prepaid call time can be as cheap as HK$50.

➡ Phonecards are available at 7-Eleven and Circle K stores.

Useful Phone Numbers

Country code ☎852
(☎853 for Macau)

International dialling code ☎001

International directory enquiries ☎10015

Local directory enquiries ☎1081

Reverse-charge/collect calls ☎10010

Tourist Information

➡ The very efficient and friendly **Hong Kong Tourism Board** (香港旅遊發展局, HKTB; ☎2508 1234; www.discoverhongkong.com) produces reams of useful pamphlets and publications. Its website is also a good point of reference.

➡ There are HKTB branches at **Hong Kong International Airport** (HKG; ☎2181 8888; www.hkairport.com), the **Star Ferry** concourse in Tsim Sha Tsui and the **Peak Piazza** (www.thepeak.com.hk; 11am-8pm) at Victoria

Peak. Alternatively, call the HKTB Visitor Hotline if you have a query or problem or if you're lost; you'll find staff eager to help.

Travellers with Disabilities

➡ Disabled people will have to cope with MTR stairs as well as pedestrian overpasses, narrow footpaths and steep hills. People whose sight or hearing is impaired must be cautious of Hong Kong's demon drivers. On the other hand, some stairs in MTR stations and most buses are now accessible by wheelchair, taxis are never hard to find, and most buildings have lifts (many with Braille panels). Wheelchairs can negotiate the lower decks of most of the ferries, and almost all public toilets now have access for the disabled.

Language

Cantonese is the most popular Chinese dialect in Hong Kong. Cantonese speakers can read Chinese characters, but will pronounce many characters differently from a Mandarin speaker.

Cantonese has 'tonal' quality – the raising and lowering of pitch on certain syllables. Tones fall on vowels and on the consonant **n**. Our pronunciation guides show five tones, indicated by accent marks – **à** (high), **á** (high rising), **à** (low falling), **á** (low rising), **a** (low) – plus a level tone (**a**).

To enhance your trip with a phrasebook, visit **lonelyplanet.com**.

Basics

Hello.	哈佬。	hàa·ló
Goodbye.	再見。	joy·gin
How are you?	你幾好啊嗎？	láy gáy hó à maa
Fine.	幾好。	gáy hó
Please ...	唔該……	ng·gòy ...
Thank you.	多謝。	dàw·je
Excuse me.	對唔住。	deui·ng·jew
Sorry.	對唔住。	deui·ng·jew
Yes.	係。	hai
No.	不係。	ng·hai

Do you speak English?
你識唔識講英文啊？　láy sìk·ng·sìk gáwng yìng·mán aa

I don't understand.
我唔明　ngáw ng mìng

Eating & Drinking

I'd like..., please.
唔該我要……　ng·gòy ngáw yiu ...

a table for two	兩位嘅檯	léung wái ge tóy
the drink list	酒料單	jáu·liú·dàan
the menu	菜單	choy·dàan
beer	啤酒	bè·jáu
coffee	咖啡	gaa·fè

I don't eat ...
我唔吃……　ngáw ng sik ...

fish	魚	yéw
poultry	雞鴨鵝	gài ngaap ngàw
red meat	牛羊肉	ngàu yèung yuk

Cheers!
乾杯！　gàwn·buì

That was delicious.
真好味。　jàn hó·may

I'd like the bill, please.
唔該我要埋單。　ng·gòy ngáw yiu màai·dàan

Shopping

I'd like to buy ...
我想買……　ngáw séung máai ...

I'm just looking.
睇下。　tái haa

How much is it?
幾多錢?　gáy·dàw chín

That's too expensive.
太貴啦 。   taai gwai laa

Can you lower the price?
可唔可以平   háw·ǹg·háw·yí pèng
啲呀 ?   dì aa

Emergencies

Help!   救命 !   gau·mèng
Go away!   走開 !   jáu·hòy

Call a doctor!
快啲叫醫生 !   faai·dì giu yì·sàng

Call the police!
快啲叫警察 !   faai·dì giu gíng·chaat

I'm lost.
我蕩失路 。   ngáw dawng·sàk·lo

I'm sick.
我病咗 。   ngáw beng·jáw

Where are the toilets?
廁所喺邊度 ?   chi·sáw hái bìn·do

Time & Numbers

What time is it?
而家   yi·gàa
幾點鐘 ?   gáy·dím·jùng

It's (10) o'clock.
(十)點鐘 。   (sap)·dím·jùng

Half past (10).
(十)點半 。   (sap)·dím bun

morning	朝早	jiù·jó
afternoon	下晝	haa·jau
evening	夜晚	ye·máan
yesterday	寢日	kàm·yat
today	今日	gàm·yat
tomorrow	听日	tìng·yat

1	一	yàt
2	二	yi
3	三	sàam
4	四	say
5	五	ńg
6	六	luk
7	七	chàt
8	八	baat
9	九	gáu
10	十	sap

Transport & Directions

Where's ...?
……喺邊度 ?   ... hái bìn·do

What's the address?
地址係 ?   day·jí hai

How do I get there?
點樣去 ?   dím·yéung heui

How far is it?
有幾遠 ?   yáu gáy yéwn

Can you show me (on the map)?
你可唔可以   láy háw·ǹg·háw·yí
(喺地圖度)指俾   (hái day·to do) jí báy
我睇我喺邊度 ?   ngáw tái ngáw hái bìn·do

When's the next bus?
下一班巴士   haa·yàt·bàan bàa·sí
幾點開 ?   gáy dím hòy

A ticket to ...
一張去……   yàt jèung heui ...
嘅飛 。   ge fày

Does it stop at ...?
會唔會喺   wuí·ǹg·wuí hái
……停呀 ?   ... tìng aa

I'd like to get off at ...
我要喺……   ngáw yiu hái ...
落車 。   lawk·chè

Behind the Scenes

Send Us Your Feedback

We love to hear from travellers – your comments help make our books better. We read every word, and we guarantee that your feedback goes straight to the authors. Visit **lonelyplanet.com/contact** to submit your updates and suggestions.

Note: We may edit, reproduce and incorporate your comments in Lonely Planet products such as guidebooks, websites and digital products, so let us know if you don't want your comments reproduced or your name acknowledged. For a copy of our privacy policy visit lonelyplanet.com/privacy.

Our Readers

Many thanks to the travellers who used the last edition and wrote to us with helpful hints, useful advice and interesting anecdotes:

Chris Lockhart, Katie Gardiner, Laura Viveros, Paul Spaeth and Raphael Isnard.

Piera's Thanks

Thanks to Ulysses, Yangi, Jackal and Antonio for making my research an exciting journey. Gratitude also goes to Janine, Lambda, Zoe and CSY for their generous assistance; and to Tina and Carmen for their kindness and company. Finally I must acknowledge my husband Sze Pang-cheung and my muse Clio for their understanding and wonderful support.

Acknowledgments

Cover photograph: Victoria Harbour from Victoria Peak; Sean Pavone/Alamy

This Book

This 5th edition of Lonely Planet's *Pocket Hong Kong* was researched and written by Piera Chen, who also wrote the previous edition. This guidebook was produced by the following:

Destination Editor Megan Eaves **Coordinating Editor** Simon Williamson **Product Editor** Kate Mathews **Senior Cartographer** Julie Sheridan **Book Designer** Virginia Moreno **Senior Editor** Karyn Noble

Assisting Editors Andi Jones, Jenna Myers **Cover Researcher** Naomi Parker **Thanks to** Joe Bindloss, Penny Cordner, Ryan Evans, Larissa Frost, Martine Power, Ellie Simpson

Index

See also separate subindexes for:

🍽 **Eating p202**

🍷 **Drinking p203**

☆ **Entertainment p203**

🛍 **Shopping p203**